PSYCHOLOGY
AND
PHYSICAL ACTIVITY

PRENTICE-HALL, INC., *London*
PRENTICE-HALL OF AUSTRALIA, PTY. LTD., *Sydney*
PRENTICE-HALL OF CANADA, LTD., *Toronto*
PRENTICE-HALL OF INDIA PRIVATE LTD., *New Delhi*
PRENTICE-HALL OF JAPAN, INC., *Tokyo*

PSYCHOLOGY
AND
PHYSICAL ACTIVITY

Bryant J. Cratty
University of California
Los Angeles, California

PRENTICE-HALL, INC., ENGLEWOOD CLIFFS, NEW JERSEY

The book is respectfully dedicated to

Dr. Donald T. Handy

Forty years prior to the publication of *Psychology and Physical Activity,* advertisements in professional journals announced the publication of *Psychology and Athletics* written by the American psychologist Coleman R. Griffith. A comparison of the two books affords some revealing insight into the events and changes that have filled the years between the respective dates of publication.

Both books were intended to bridge the gap between science and the day-to-day practices of physical educators and coaches. Both authors drew upon their knowledge of the research literature in behavioral psychology. Both books contained statements that were intended to reflect a consensus of evidence with regard to a variety of factors related to the acquisition and performance of motor skills. Both authors were aware of severe limitations within the body of knowledge available to them and both men held their conclusions to be entirely tentative and contingent upon future research. Finally, both authors displayed the courage required of a scholar who wishes to step out of his familiar and comfortable role as scientist, to make intuitive and often daring leaps beyond the immediate limits of available data to the domain of implications for practice.

The two books differ most in terms of substance contained. The explosion of research and scholarly writing provided, on the one hand, a vastly richer starting point for Professor Cratty. On the other hand, in topic areas

Foreword

which Griffith could exhaust with a few citations, Cratty was confronted with difficult problems of organization and selection.

Of greater import are differences that lie not in the books, the authors, or the body of knowledge, but in the audiences which the books address. While Griffith's book is still cherished by some, it never achieved wide acceptance or exerted notable influence upon its audience of teachers and coaches. Physical educators and coaches were not ready in 1928 to think of themselves, their students, or their subject matter as illuminated in any fruitful way by the work of behavioral scientists.

In contrast, the present book will reach an audience that believes, perhaps too fervently, that research either does or should play a significant role in shaping professional practice. Teachers and coaches are now quite ready to look to behavioral science for guidelines that increase the probability of making effective professional decisions and that enrich their repertoire of alternative pedagogical strategies.

Professor Cratty's bibliographies provide ideal entry points into a body of literature that is difficult for the newcomer to penetrate. The organization of major topics, summary statements, and corollaries provide a rough but utilitarian structure for what might otherwise appear to be a highly recondite collection of disparate facts and theories.

Whatever virtues the book may have, none can compare with its unique value as a tool for the development and dissemination of practices based upon research. However tentative and unsatisfactory we may find the present links between behavioral science and professional practice, there is no alternative to the business of constructing those links. Attempts to bridge the gap between theory and practice always draw fire from the purists on either side. Such is the lot of the middleman. Professor Cratty's work rings too true as both disciplined scholarship and practical professionalism to be punctured by casual critics. This book will be read and, of far greater importance, *used* by a new generation of men and women whose subject matter is physical activity.

LAWRENCE F. LOCKE
Teachers College
Columbia University

Contents

part one

THE INDIVIDUAL PERFORMS

The response capabilities of the individual are dependent upon his innate neuromotor makeup, his physical structure, and his typical level of activation, as well as his inclination to move at a given moment in a given task. An overriding principle is that an individual cannot perform at a level higher than that permitted by the response capacities of his nervous system. For example, the speed of conduction of the nerve impulse limits reaction time, while the speed with which one can integrate visual and kinesthetic input limits, to some degree, the complexity of rapid movements in which one can engage.

Evolution also influences the individual's capacity to respond. Manipulative abilities are probably superior to mental-motor integrations because of their earlier appearance on the phylogenic scale. Many early primates had opposable thumbs between 20 and 40 million years ago. Effective locomotion and the integration of thought with movement, on the other hand, cause more problems, and are probably less refined than they will be eons of years in the future. Upright walking emerged in pre-men about two to three million years ago, while man's present brain size is a relatively recent innovation, appearing only about 50,000 years ago.

These evolutionary characteristics of the human action system and its sub-systems mold man's response capabilities. Movements made in front of the body, due to the frequent pairing of vision and manipulation, are far more accurate than movements in other posi-

1 Basic Performance

tions of the individual's space field. The movements of the upper limbs are far more refined than those of the lower limbs.

Vision and, to some degree, verbal behavior permeate most facets of man's movement attributes. Sub-vocal movements of the lips may accompany "silent" reading. Most people engage in internal verbalizing when confronted with a motor task. Heightening the general tension of an individual by the squeezing of a hand grip has been found to facilitate the mental learning of a series of words and letters. Therefore it is difficult, and at times impossible, to separate mental, verbal, and motor behaviors into separate niches.

We have, however, attempted to focus attention upon the response mechanisms, primarily those controlled by the larger muscles of the body. The interrelationships among perception, vision, verbal ability, and other aspects of the human personality will become apparent in the chapters which follow.

The less complex characteristic responses of the individual will be considered initially: response time, reaction time, movement speed and strength. Following the statements related to reaction time and movement speed, material related to more complex coordinations is presented.

Reaction time may be defined as time between presentation of a stimulus and initiation of the response. It includes nerve conduction time for both incoming and outgoing impulses, and also the time necessary to integrate input and output within the central nervous system.

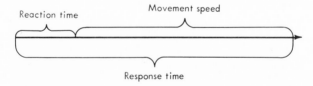

Fig. 1. Movement Speed, Reaction Time, and Response Time. Response time is measured from the time the stimulus for action appears (i.e., the starter's gun explodes) until the time the movement is initiated. Movement speed is measured from the beginning of some action until its conclusion. Response time is sometimes used to denote the combined time of both reaction time and movement speed.

If the movement initiated has involved integration by the central nervous system, i.e., a conscious decision made, it is usually found that the reaction time is slower; in this situation, reaction time and judgment time are difficult to separate. It is perhaps better to consider a continuum from simple reaction time to a prolonged period of time during which the individual makes a conscious and careful decision concerning the action to be carried out.

Movement speed is generally defined as the time taken for a movement to occur, from its initiation to its termination. Response time is a broader term, inclusive of both movement speed and reaction time. There are, of course, innumerable situations in sports and physical education when it is desirable to train individuals to respond more rapidly. Specific implications follow these statements.

1.0 *Reaction time is dependent upon the characteristics of the stimuli as well as upon various characteristics of the individual responding* (10).

Corollary 1.1   In general, if the intensity of the stimulus is increased, reaction time will be shortened (10).

People will react more quickly, to a point, to a louder noise, a brighter color, and a sharper command. If a point is exceeded, however, the intense stimuli will tend to block performance, because of their stressful nature.

Corollary 1.2   The nature of the stimuli will also influence reaction time. Individuals react quicker to an auditory stimulus than to a visual stimulus (1).

Corollary 1.3   The mental "set" of the individual, whether he is attentive or inattentive, will affect reaction time in the expected direction (6).

A heightened state of tension and arousal will shorten reaction time. If a sprinter awaiting the starter's gun is thinking "move" rather than simply listening for the noise, his reaction time is likely to be longer.

Implications.   In tasks in which it is desirable to shorten reaction time, as in the start of short races or the initial charge by the football lineman, the coach should attempt to exactly duplicate the stimulus conditions in practice in order to elicit the greatest transfer to the actual game situation. At the same time, he should instruct his players in the proper mental set. That is, he might heighten their state of alertness by verbal exhortation. An attempt should also be made to induce mental set relative to the type of sensory information to which the performer must react in the game situation. Waterpolo and basketball practices should be officiated during the week so that the players will react to the proper auditory stimulus (whistle) and visual stimuli (flags and/or hand signals) to which they will be expected to react in the game.

The shorter the races in which a runner is participating, the greater the percentage of time that should be devoted to specific reaction-time drills. Similarly, in team games the players should be taught to respond quickly to the multitude of conditions which trigger action. In basketball, for example, teams should be taught to react quickly when the ball falls through the hoop as they are scored upon. Specific drills should be initiated by such stimuli in these team endeavors.

Corollary 1.4   Reaction time will be shorter when it is known that a simpler response is to be called for. When a signal is to be followed by a complex response, reaction time is generally prolonged (6).

Implications. This corollary suggests that when a complex response is required to a stimulus, the prolonged reaction time may be more disruptive of performance. Reaction time may be improved only to a point which is roughly determined by the response capacity of the neuromotor system. The greatest improvement in reaction time may therefore be expected by "programming" the complex movement so that the amount of input and output time (stimulus and movement) can be shortened. Thus, reaction time may be shortened by practicing the complex movements required following various kinds of stimuli. Quickly jumping out of bounds with the basketball, following a whistle and/or arm signal by the official, for example, should be practiced until nearly automatic in order that the responding team may "get the jump" on their opponents. Practice will be most likely to elicit improvement in reaction times occurring prior to more complex movements.

2.0   *Movement speed is relatively independent of reaction time, moderately related to strength, and influenced positively in roughly the same way as is reaction time (7, 8).*

In general, moderate increases in movement speed will result if players are engaged in proper training. The most effective way to improve movement speed is through practice. Verbal reinforcement and other intense stimuli have been found to improve movement speed. Thus shouting by the performer can be expected to improve his movement speed and his striking capacity if the limb encounters an opponent's chin.

Although it has been assumed at times that a practiced act becomes "automatic" and, by inference, reflex-like, contemporary neurological evidence suggests that all movements originally learned under voluntary control remain under the control of the cortex. Movement speed, nevertheless, can be increased to a point at which no apparent delay is noted between the stimulus and the subsequent action. Most improvement in skilled performance is dependent upon movement speed rather than shortened reaction time; some authorities suggest that initial practice at almost full speed is essential, even though resulting in inaccurate performance, in order to enhance final speed and accuracy.

Emphasis should probably be placed upon the speed of a complex movement during the terminal stages of learning a complex task. At times, however, initial "speed stress" by a coach-teacher can so disrupt perform-ance that other initial components of the task—its spatial dimensions and mechanical principles—may become obliterated, and learning is impeded.

Improvement in the movement speed components of a complex task requiring rapid responses is the primary way in which the total action pattern is enhanced. For example, goal tending in ice hockey, soccer, waterpolo, and similar sports will be improved not so much by attempting to improve the individual's reaction time to the stimulus represented by the puck or ball, but by practice in all of the specific physical actions required to intercept the ball.

> **3.0** *The specificity of motor skill is dependent upon the nature of the individuals compared, the amount of past experience they have had in a number of skills, and the extent to which they can profit from their past experiences.*

Corollary 3.1 In a group of mature people similar in background, motor skill is seen to be highly specific (3).

Attempting to predict the performance of an individual on a given task by reference to his score on another task is usually difficult.

Implications. When working with groups of adolescents who are intelligent and stable emotionally, one must practice the specifics of the task one desires them to learn in order to obtain best results. The task's spatial dimensions and velocities, as well as specific applications of force, must be integrated into the learning process. Expecting transfer from a "coordination task" to the primary task in question will not be as pro-ductive as practicing the specific components of the task desired for mastery. For example, it is faulty reasoning for the basketball coach to expect some "general coordination" task to aid defensive ability in basket-ball more than would the specific components of footwork needed on defense.

In a population of experienced, relatively intelligent people, a factoral analysis fragments strength into three components (static, explosive, and dynamic strength), balance into four components (balancing objects, bal-ancing statically with and without vision, and moving while balancing with vision); manual skill is divisible into from five to seven components; flexibility is likewise factorable into flexibility while moving rapidly and slow "extent" flexibility.

Thus, coordination drills are best if they approximate exactly the move-ments of the sport to which they are applied. Although there is some tendency for individuals to become generally oriented to learning various agility tasks quickly, more rapid improvement will be made by intelligent individuals free from perceptual-motor defects if they are asked to practice the specific tasks or task components related to the final skill it is wished to improve.

Further implications of this marked specificity of skill suggest that one must analyze the discrete factors in the task at hand prior to attempting to devise constructive and productive sub-skills to practice. As we will see later in studying transfer, being "almost" correct when analyzing a complex skill may lead to impeding the performance of the task it is desired to improve.

Corollary 3.2   Analyses of skills in groups of young children, of children who evidence motor handicaps, and of the mentally retarded, reveal more general qualities of movement underlying performance in a number of tasks (2).

This corollary suggests that, with such groups, simpler programs of movement education might prove productive. Such programs might include training in four or five different types of tasks, including agility, balance, strength-endurance, and flexibility, and perceptual training including body-part identification and ball handling. Due to absence of a variety of past experiences, i.e., as when dealing with young children or with the inability to profit from and remember past experience of the mentally retarded, the performance of individuals in such groups appears more dependent upon inherent qualities of their neuromotor makeup than upon past experience.

The mentally retarded can be taught to think more effectively through the correct introduction and application of movement experiences. While their ability to perform motor skills is usually somewhat impaired because of their tendency to evidence concomitant defects in the neuromotor makeup, as well as inability to select appropriate work-methods when attempting complex skills, with practice many retarded children can achieve performances in motor skills nearly approximating those of normal children. Critical in the motor training of retarded and neurologically handicapped children is the introduction of activities to enhance their body image, including tasks to improve their perceptions of their body parts, the relationship of their bodies to objects in space, and various left-right discriminations relative to their bodies and to spatial objects.

4.0   *Factors at three levels influence the final characteristics of the final performance output: basic behavioral supports, physical ability traits, and, finally, the specific characteristics of the skill.*

Such basic qualities as aspiration level, ability to analyze mechanical principles, control and regulation of tension, and persistence in tasks are some of the components of human personality which form a basis for both intellectual and perceptual-motor functioning. At the intermediate level, such basic physical ability traits as static and dynamic strength influence performance in a number of tasks. At the final level, the specifics of the skill, and the unique practice conditions under which it was learned, influence output.

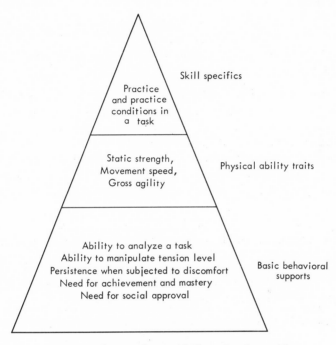

Fig. 2. A Three-Level Pyramid Illustrating Factors That Influence Perceptual-Motor Behavior.

These three levels of factors are mutually dependent. For example, success in the task itself "feeds back" into the basic level of behavior supports and raises the individual's aspiration level. His aspiration level in turn encourages him to participate more in the successful activity, and this participation contributes in turn to the development of basic ability traits.

These basic supports of behavior influence more than just the perceptual-motor functioning of the individual; they are reflected in his performance in a number of kinds of mental and perceptual tasks. Physical ability traits at the intermediate level are influential only of motor ability. The mutual influence of these three levels of factors will become clearer upon reviewing Part Three, *Motivation,* Part Five, *Learning,* and Part Six, *Group Interaction.*

> **5.0**   *A specific pattern of action of a man may be arranged on various scales denoting complexity, the amount of thought accompanying the movement, and the amount of verbal behavior and visual monitoring involved during performance of the task.*

Corollary 5.1   A shift on some of these scales occurs as the skill is learned. For example, less visual monitoring is usually needed as a skill is acquired, and less verbal behavior and thought accompany a complex action which has been practiced (3, 6).

The instructor should be sensitive to the position on a child's individual scales where a particular skill resides, and, second, to shifts on the various scales as learning takes place. For example, to a child with little experience, a particular skill will reside toward the visual end of a visual-motor scale, denoting that he usually depends upon visual inspection of his movements during the initial stages of learning. As learning progresses he depends less upon vision and more upon the kinesthetic "feel" of limb and body positions to govern the accuracy of the action. Careful observation of children as they learn motor skills should serve to inform the instructor when such shifts occur, and he may thus govern his teaching methodology accordingly.

Corollary 5.2   The designation of a skill as "complex" depends upon the maturity and past experience of the individual attempting it.

Implications.   Many of the implications arising from the above statement and its corollaries relate to the teaching and learning process, and are discussed more thoroughly in Part Five, *Learning.* In general, however, it must be remembered that an individual, as he practices a skill, is varying the manner in which he integrates various components of his behavior during the learning process. Initially he must think about the task, and understand its spatial dimensions and, if he is capable, its mechanical principles. The coach-instructor should therefore aid him in this initial process of understanding by supplementing the information the learner may be attempting to obtain from observing the nature of the task. During the final stages of learning, the performer's progress can be impeded by inappropriate or unnecessary interference from the coach-teacher in the form of too many verbal instructions.

> **6.0**   *The performance of many sports skills may be influenced by innate reflex patterns. (9).*

Corollary 6.1   **Certain basic reflexes enhance the performance of various skills.**

A basic extension reflex is involved when the legs and arms are vigorously extended at the same time. When jumping, diving, pushing off the side of a swimming pool when turning, and otherwise desiring to elicit powerful leg drive, placing emphasis upon a vigorous extension of the arms will enhance the force of the movement. Breaststrokers find that they snap their legs together harder in the kick if they thrust their arms vigorously forward at the same time.

Shot-putters are usually observed to thrust their heads to the left when vigorously extending their right arms in the final thrusting action. This is probably indicative of the involvement of the tonic-neck reflex.

The side stroke is relatively easy to learn because of the similarity of the voluntary pattern required to the cross-extension reflex which underlies walking and crawling. The bottom arm extends while the top leg does the same during the power phase of the sidestroke.

Certain movements in various sports must be given more practice than others. Those which almost duplicate normal reflex patterns, and which seem to "fall into place," will require less instruction to enhance the integration of limbs and applications of force. On the other hand, those tasks which oppose "natural" reflexive movements will require more careful rehearsal, particularly during the initial stages of learning.

Corollary 6.2   **The performance and learning of other sports skills may be impeded because they are in opposition to basic reflexive patterns.**

A fly-away from the horizontal bar (back somersault off on the front swing) opposes a general extension pattern. The performer, when learning, is usually attempting to execute a vigorous flexion of his lower limbs; the knees are brought quickly to the chest, while at the same time the arms must be kept straight and the hands extended as he releases the bar. Since it is easier to extend or flex all parts of the body at the same time, learning this movement is sometimes impeded because of its opposition to a general extension reflex. The coordination in the breaststroke is similarly difficult, since the upper part of the body is generally extended while the legs are flexing prior to executing the kick.

The coach should determine whether a movement opposes or corresponds to some of the innate reflexes of the body and, when possible, attempt to design the execution of the skill to conform to these basic patterns. When this is not possible, the athlete should be given prolonged practice in the movement required.

It would also appear that more force could be elicited in various exercise movements if apparatus were designed to fall within various reflexive patterns used by humans. For example, isometric exercises designed to improve leg strength could be made more effective if the arms were involved simultaneously in static positions appropriate to the kind of strength desired. If leg extension force is desired, it would seem proper to place the arms in a manner which would also enable them to apply force in extended positions.

Summary

Identification of factors which contribute to final skilled output is dependent upon the manner in which a number of skills are analyzed, the bias of the experimenter as he selects skills to be studied, and the intellectual and physical makeup of the individuals studied. Recent investigations have uncovered innumerable factors which contribute to what were previously considered "basic" factors. These kinds of analyses have suggested that, through more careful examination of the nature of the complex tasks within various sports and the careful designing of exercises and drills to enhance basic qualities, we might expect our athletes of the future to become more proficient.

Trunk strength seems to underlie the performance of a number of motor skills. Strength of the midsection and lower back appears to be imperative, insofar as the body "hinge" needs to be stable when throwing, running, or otherwise involving the limbs in various activities.

Speed of movement seems to be a rather general quality present in both arm and leg movements which is, of course, necessary in a number of skilled acts, and, at the same time, apparently highly trainable. Speed of bodily movement, i.e., agility, seems somewhat independent of speed of limb movement, and is related to balance and dynamic strength. The relative independence of strength and speed, however, suggests that if some kind of weight training is given preparatory to athletic performances which require rapid movements, training should include movements which, although "overloaded," could be rapid and similar in quality to those desired in the sports skill.

Recent research indicated the importance of the perceptual components of the motor act. Almost all complex voluntary actions of man are heavily dependent upon the manner in which the performer organizes sensory information received from kinesthetic receptors, visual apparatus, and balance mechanism. Failure to recognize the unique characteristics of the situation and the way in which they contribute to the individual's performance omits an important dimension in the learning of skills. A more detailed analysis of perception and perceptual training is found in Part Four.

Raising an individual's tension level will positively contribute to the performance of simple reaction time-movement time speed tasks; if the tension is increased past a given point it will detract from performance in complex movements. A thorough discussion of this theory is found in Part Three.

Social stimulation, or lack of it, at the time the individual performs has been consistently demonstrated to exert significant influence upon levels of performance in both complex and forceful acts. The mere presence of an onlooker can alter tension level, which in turn changes motoric output. Competing and otherwise interacting with other individuals during performance exerts even more marked influences upon individual effort. Part Six contains more detailed information concerning the manner in which various social situations and factors influence perceptual-motor performance.

The teacher-coach will become more effective if, instead of considering each skilled act within a framework of his own choosing, he considers the manner in which the learner confronting him may view the situation. He will be successful, in essence, to the extent to which he is able to "get inside the skin" of the members of his class. Important to developing this sensitivity is gaining an awareness of how children of both sexes, and of various ages, perform and are affected by changes in social stimulation, group interaction, and various sub-cultures with which they are constantly in contact (e.g., their families). Part Two, *Maturation*, contains principles which hopefully will heighten the reader's sensitivity to the influence of various maturational differences upon perceptual-motor functioning.

Throughout the ensuing pages, examples are presented which relate to sports skills, developmental programs for children, and activities common to physical education classes. It is, of course, beyond the scope of any book to outline in detail all the situations in which some of these findings may be operative. It is believed that the reader will profit from the material contained within this text to the extent that he can successfully apply the statements to the variety of situations which he will encounter during his teaching and coaching career.

Virtually every confrontation between two people is followed by some kind of behavioral change. Although it would seem that the primary purpose of the text is to create an attitude in the teacher-coach which encourages merely a rapid mental shuffling of a multitude of variables, such is not the case. Teachers and coaches must *act,* and in supportive, positive ways. Indeed, inaction on their part can have a critical impact on those in their charge. Therefore, the materials which follow are primarily intended to outline purposeful courses of action for the teacher-coach; they are also intended to suggest helpful alternatives of behavior in which the instructor can engage as he becomes better able to assess the situation, the nature of the learner, and himself. As a result of these assessments, he may engage in more productive behavior, and in turn elicit better performance from those he leads.

Athletic teams in competition and physical education classes interacting are heavily charged with situations that have emotional overtones. Change will always occur on the part of the participants in these programs. It is hoped that the reader will gain from a survey of these materials and guide the nature of that change in positive directions.

BIBLIOGRAPHY

1. Costa, L. D., Rapid, I., and Mandel, I. J. Two experiments in visual and auditory reaction time in children at a school for the deaf. *Percept. and Mot. Skills,* 1964, 19, 291.

2. Cratty, Bryant J. *Developmental sequences of perceptual-motor tasks.* Freeport, N.Y.: Educational Activities, Inc., 1967.

3. Fitts, Paul M., and Posner, M. I. *Human performance.* Belmont, Calif.: Brooks/Cole Publishing Company, 1967.

4. Fleishman, Edwin A. Factorial analysis of complex psychomotor performance and related skills. *J. Applied Psychol.,* 1956, 40, 2.

5. Fleishman, Edwin A., and Hempel, Walter E., Jr. Changes in factor structure of a complex psychomotor test as a function of practice. *Psychometrike,* 1954, 19, 239–252.

6. Henry, F. M. Increased response latency for complicated movements and a "memory drum" theory of neuromotor reaction. *Res. Quart.,* 1960, 31, 448–457.

7. ———. Independence of reaction and movement times and equivalence of sensory motivators of fast response. *Res. Quart.,* 1952, 23, 43–53.

8. Henry, Franklin, and Whitley, J. D. Relationships between individual differences in strength, speed and mass in an arm movement. *Res. Quart.,* 1960, 31, 24–33.

9. Peiper, Albrecht. *Cerebral function in infancy and childhood.* Chapter 4: Reflexes of position and movement. New York: The International Behavioral Sciences Series, Consultants Bureau, 1963.

10. Teichner, W. H. Recent studies of simple reaction time. *Psychol. Bull.,* 1954, 51, 128–145.

11. Woodson, W. E., and Conover, D. W. *Human engineering.* Berkeley: University of California Press, 1964.

Relationships between personality and performance in athletic skills are often discussed in the pages of professional journals and by individuals on the playing field. People placed in situations which call for action usually reveal more of themselves than is exposed in less dynamic situations. Some have speculated that movement characteristics underlie many of the traits of the total personality complex.

The term *personality* has many meanings, but in general its usage is based upon the assumption that there are consistencies in behavior which are evidenced by an individual in a variety of situations. Personality denotes the total behavioral pattern of a person and is usually experimentally divided into traits denoting values, intellect, emotional makeup, and, at times, perceptual-motor attributes.

Experimental efforts to clarify personality-performance relationships are sometimes superficial. Frequently only a few subjects are used; at other times, personality scales with which the experimenters have had little experience are employed. Conclusions not justified by the findings have often been stated. For example, upon finding that athletes possess personality traits different from non-athletes, it is usually implied that athletic competition has *caused* the differences, rather than a speculation that individuals with certain personality characteristics may simply tend to direct their energies toward sports participation. A longitudinal study comparing personality changes of athletes and non-athletes,

2 Personality and Performance

when both groups were exposed to competitive athletics from their seventeenth to twenty-first years, indicated that the trait differences of the two groups remained fixed during this period of time. Thus it might be assumed that, at least by the age of seventeen, boys already know their real capabilities in competing with peers, and artificial attempts to achieve personality trait changes by exposure to athletic competition following this age will meet with little success (21).

The individual physique is intimately related to the study of personality and performance. The physique is essentially the vehicle with which an individual performs. Feelings of self-confidence or lack of assurance may thus stem from the negative or positive reactions an individual receives from others as they assess performance potential by inspecting his bodily characteristics.

Movements which communicate are also linked to the study of personality and performance. The gestures, posturings, and facial expressions which accompany verbal communication are cues through which people give meaning to the emotions, thoughts, and feelings they attempt to transmit to one another (14).

On the following pages, personality and motor performance will be explored from three standpoints: (a) relationships between specific personality traits and levels of skill, (b) physique and personality, and (c) individual differences reflecting consistencies in movement speed, persistence, and space used when performing motor tasks.

7.0   *As individuals gain status for successful performance of tasks valued by a group, they become more outgoing, less anxious, and more self-confident (12).*

Corollary 7.1   Athletic success by boys in childhood and adolescence enhances their self-esteem. Physical ineptitude accompanies feelings of inferiority (11).

Corollary 7.2   Late maturing males often have feelings of inferiority (12).

Corollary 7.3   Early maturing males perform physical skills best in early adolescence and evidence feelings of superiority (12).

Implications. The statement and corollaries suggest that early maturation is important both to the achievement of success in highly valued skills and to the assumption of personality traits accompanying this status. It is usually suggested that improving a boy's performance in skills enhances certain personality traits.

These principles suggest that the physical educator should attempt to plan programs so that boys of equal skills (i.e., of equal maturational levels, rather than similar chronological ages) are grouped together for competition. At the same time, it seems imperative for instructors to be sensitive to the late maturing and/or inept boy in their programs, and attempt to raise his level of skill to a point which will enable him to reach minimal levels of group acceptance by his peers.

The available evidence indicates that although personality traits of "good" versus "poor" performers remain relatively fixed after 17 or 18, the influence of athletic success or lack of success on personality takes place during childhood and early adolescence (21). During these years it is probable that the coach and physical educator can exert a great influence upon the personalities of boys in their charge by enhancing their feelings about their levels of performance in motor skills as well as the skill itself.

The physical educator cannot manipulate the age at which a boy matures. On the other hand, he *can* decide which boys compete with one another, and to some degree can change the skill levels of the late maturing and/or unskilled performer.

There are innumerable ways in which a physical education teacher can "protect" the personalities of less skilled individuals in his charge. It is still a frequent practice, for example, to select teams when class members are gathered together, making it painfully clear which individuals are highly prized and which are rejected by the group. A more positive way of accomplishing this is to select the teams from the class roll book, so that the class members have no knowledge of the order in which they were selected. Even more desirable is to have four team captains select teams from the roll book, and then have the captains draw lots to determine which of the teams they will lead! Such a practice should certainly serve to establish teams of equal ability, and at the same time prevent inferior performers from continuing to be subjected to negative appraisals from their peers.

The simple cause-effect relationship between personality change and athletic performance has not been demonstrated by any experimental evidence known to the writer. One can make as good a case for the hypothesis that boys with certain personality complexes seek athletic participation, as for the assumption that athletic participation changes personality. Indeed, the evidence cited above suggests that, after the ages of 17 and 18, athletic participation does not significantly alter the personality structure of either the athlete or the non-athlete. Whether or not an individual participates in athletics is not as important as his *feelings* about his levels of performance as related to his perceptions of acceptable performance achievable by others of his age and sex. Chapter 3 relates in more detail the concept of *aspiration level.*

> **8.0**   There are certain consistencies in the manner in which an individual may perform several kinds of motor tasks.

Corollary 8.1   "Persistence" seems to underlie the performance of various skills. An individual's willingness to endure discomfort molds his performance in both motor and mental tasks, particularly under conditions which involve some kind of social stimulation (15).

Implications. Several studies suggest that individuals who tend to persist in one task can be expected to continue to work hard in another even when subjected to some kind of discomfort. A coach might devise screening tests which would enable him to predict team dropouts prior to beginning the season, e.g., by asking a boy to engage in various static positioning tasks and noting how long he is willing to continue. Another commonly used experimental task is to request the subject to maintain one half his maximum grip strength on a hand dynometer, and to note the time he is willing to do so (15).

Essentially, such measures evaluate the individual's ability to withstand pain and discomfort, both concomitants of athletic performance at the highly competitive levels. At the same time, the indication that a given individual will not persist well in uncomfortable tasks is not an indication of a character deficiency, simply a signpost that he must be handled differently when being conditioned in athletic skills.

There is no direct evidence that training of boys to persist for periods of time in endurance activities, represented by distance swimming and running, will extend tolerance to psychological fatigue in mental tasks. However, there is no reason to believe that this kind of carry-over might not take place.

Tenacity is a personality quality highly valued in students by instructors of physical activities as well as by classroom teachers. The experimental literature suggests that tenacity is predictable by evaluation of an individual's behavior when exposed to relatively simple experimental tasks.

Corollary 8.2   The amount of space an individual habitually utilizes in specific kinds of tasks seems predictable within limits. In relatively unstructured situations, some people habitually utilize large amounts of space, while others are relatively restricted in their actions (1).

Implications. Teachers of dance are primarily concerned with this performance quality, and a recent study demonstrates that there are consistent individual differences in the willingness to utilize space when moving the total body to music in the absence of specific instructions. It is suggested that some students need to be placed in situations and given instructions which are designed to encourage them to use more space in the movements they evidence.

Various programs designed to enhance muscular relaxation might accompany programs of dance and similar activities in which it is desired that an individual utilize varying amounts of space with his movements. Children's movement education programs, in which it is requested that they "make themselves as large (or as small) as they can" or that they utilize movements in a large (or a small) amount of space, are helpful. If such tasks are administered at early ages, they should result in individuals who are perceptually flexible enough to accommodate the spatial requirements of more structured tasks in late childhood and early adolescence.

It is felt that many children in early adolescence exhibit restricted and tense movements because they suffer feelings of inferiority about their changing bodies. Research is lacking concerning the exact parameters of the relationships between these hypothesized feelings and the spatial qualities of their movements. However, the extent to which adolescents are comfortable with the size and shape of their bodies, and their willingness to engage in a variety of movement tasks, particularly those involving large amounts of space, are apparently closely related.

This same "extent of movement" quality seems present in certain highly structured tasks. For example, individuals asked to draw "four-inch lines" will usually draw lines longer than four inches; upon being asked to draw "15-inch lines," they will inscribe a line shorter than requested (3). Similarly, when asked to make facing movements without vision or sound cues, people habitually turn more than the requested 90 degrees, while underturning full turns requested by 40 degrees (8)! Thus, there seems to be, in various situations, an amount of space individuals prefer to use which is relatively independent of the instructions given to them. Sensitivity to these inclinations in sports performers and dancers should result in more effective communication between teacher and pupil, and quicker change in the behavior of the latter.

Corollary 8.3   Preferred speed of movement underlies the performance of a number of motor activities. Several investigators have isolated general factors relating to preferred speed of movement by surveying performance of tapping rate and similar tasks in which care was taken to avoid encouraging the subjects to exhibit maximum speed (16).

Implications. Although preferred speed and all-out capacity for rapid movement are not highly correlated, the available literature suggests that, in relatively unstructured situations, an individual will tend to move at a preferred rate of speed which may also be reflected in other motor activities. Dance teachers, in particular, must at times break through this characteristic of their pupils in order to elicit desired variations in rhythm. Cognizance of this individual tendency, it is believed, should enhance teacher-pupil rapport in a number of situations.

Children of all ages should be encouraged to duplicate a number of kinds of rhythms with their bodily movements. Tasks requiring rapid transition from one movement speed to another should be incorporated into programs of dance and physical education. At the advanced levels children should be asked to duplicate various syncopated rhythms, and to duplicate one rhythmic pattern with one part of their body while duplicating another rhythm simultaneously with another part.

> **9.0** Certain combinations of personality traits have been shown to be predictive of superior performance in various athletic endeavors as well as in certain skills within the experimental laboratory (7).

The writer has found that a group of personality traits which reflected freedom from agitation, high need for social approval, and lack of hostility to the environment was predictive of successful performance in complex tasks involving accurate movements of the total body (7).

Implications. More and more coaches of professional teams in the major spectator sports are requesting that trait analyses of their players be made prior to their selection as regulars. High school coaches continually make subjective judgments concerning the personality traits of their team members, e.g., is he "mean enough to play tackle?" While it is an expensive and complex undertaking for the average high school coach to obtain a personality profile of prospective team members, ignoring the role of personality in the selection of the starting line-up will lead to less effective team performance.

The successful coach should not only observe the obvious performance characteristics of his players, but also look more closely to discover how they feel about sports participation, how they react to stresses of various kinds, and how they behave in situations other than those faced on the athletic field. In other ways, we should attempt to understand the total personality of the athlete in our charge. The exactitude with which these assessments are accomplished, it is believed, will determine the degree of success that can be expected from the collective efforts of the team members.

Changes in personality as a result of success or failure in the athletic situation should also be taken into account. Some athletes take a loss exceedingly hard, and must be bolstered back into action after such a setback. Others tend to gloss too lightly over a loss, and may not examine thoroughly the reasons for their failure to do well.

The influence of various dominant personalities upon less forceful members of teams should also be assessed. A boy's personality does not develop in a vacuum, but is a reflection of the situations and individuals with which he is confronted. The harmful and helpful influences of various personalities upon one another in a team situation should be constantly assessed by the sensitive coach and physical education teacher.

10.0   *Certain personality traits have been demonstrated to be predictive of athletic activities which individuals select.*

Generally, research corroborates the common observation that individual-sports athletes tend to be more withdrawn, while team-sports athletes tend to be more gregarious. At the same time, personality traits other than those which might be expected are uncovered upon polling individuals in various sports activities. For example, the writer, after administering an anxiety questionnaire to several activity classes over a period of years, noted with surprise that consistently high scores were obtained from boys who selected diving. It seemed that these boys may have chosen a "brave looking" sport to construct a facade of courage which in truth they did not feel in themselves (5).

Implications.   The possibility of screening populations for personality types best suited to various sports has already been suggested. On the other hand, if personality and sport selection seem to match, a scale of game choices which attempts to evaluate certain personality traits through the individuals' inclinations towards selected sports activities might be also constructed. Such a scale has already been utilized to evaluate the degree of masculinity and femininity present in the personalities of young children (17, 19).

Sensitivity to the relationship between sports selected and personality should enable the coach-teacher to deal more effectively with boys presenting themselves for participation. The instructor might ask himself whether boys are interested in participation in the sport at hand for its own sake, or merely to bolster some perceived personality deficiency. Usually it is a combination of both reasons that prompts people to choose to participate in various athletic endeavors.

11.0   *Individuals accompany verbal communication with movements which contribute in subtle and exact ways to the information transmitted* (14).

Corollary 11.1   Movements which transmit strong emotions are probably innate, while gestures which accompany less intense verbal communication are probably learned (19).

Corollary 11.2   The social context, as well as quantitative aspects of the communicative movements (i.e., face, limbs, and/or posturing of the total body), influence the exactitude with which movements transmit ideas (14).

Implications.   It is rare for two or more individuals to confront one another without evidencing gestures which communicate information.

Teachers and coaches sensitive to this "movement communication" by the "silent" groups confronting them can increase their teaching effectiveness. Coaches are often more intent upon *telling*, rather than *listening*. At times listening can be more effectively accomplished by the eyes than by the ears.

12.0   *Individuals often behave according to the commonly held stereotype for one of their physique type (18, 20).*

Corollary 12.1   Individuals who possess bodily characteristics which denote action engage in more muscular and social activity; they tend to act as expected by those with whom they come in contact (20).

Although the prediction of *exact* personality traits is not possible from assessment of physique characteristics, it is usually noted that individuals with muscular frames tend to seek situations in which they may use their physical prowess.

Implications. The situations in which the muscular individual may seek to place himself will sometimes have asocial overtones; e.g., he may engage in delinquent behavior. It seems imperative for the physical educator-coach to recruit individuals who obviously possess the physical equipment for either destructive or constructive behavior and channel them into socially approved sports activities. Although the theory that physical activity may be successfully utilized for the draining of hostilities is open to serious question, it does seem that the capacity for action impels some people to seek action in rather direct ways. Failure to provide socially approved outlets can often lead to unfortunate consequences.

All teachers who have worked with boys in programs to improve their physical attributes and physiques can attest to the change seen in personality as a result of a positive change in the child's perceptions of himself in physical activities. Although definitive studies concerning this kind of change are presently lacking, it is reasonable to assume that, as a child is given increased evidence of his improved prowess and body-build, he will tend to act in a more positive, outgoing manner within his peer group. Conversely, as a child is given continued social feedback concerning his ineptitude and poor physique, a change in personality will occur in the opposite direction; he will become more withdrawn, and begin to evidence feelings of inferiority about himself and his physical endeavors.

Corollary 12.2   Thin people engage more in intellectual endeavors and are less outgoing socially.

The thin-withdrawn dichotomy is familiar to all, and although the relationship is not as clear as several experimenters would have us believe, knowledge of this stereotype by spare individuals probably shapes their behavior to some degree (18).

Implications. In situations which call for vigorous action special attention should be paid to boys who obviously lack the physique to perform effectively. Sensitivity to the problems of the thin and the inept performer should result in the development of a special situation in which he might be exposed to extra practice in skills and compete with others of his capacity level. Muscle size is moderately related to strength, while strength is related to success in a number of vigorous sports skills. Although some researchers suggest that physique is rather fixed, gym instructors encouraging body building have observed that marked muscular changes, involving significant shifts in physique type, may be elicited by progressive resistance exercise. It thus might be suggested that the thin boy, who may have withdrawn socially because of his feelings of physical inferiority, might be helped to achieve more successful personal adjustment by exposure to muscle building activities.

Corollary 12.3   Some adults and adolescents may attempt to bolster their personality structure by engaging in muscle building activities (10).

Implications. Body building is one of the few ways in which young men can exert their "maleness" in our society. If not carried to the point where extreme narcissism is evidenced, it is probably a relatively desirable personality support for many individuals. Boys who seem to have problems in identifying with masculine activities might be encouraged in this direction. A youth who evidences too marked a fixation upon the development of his own body should probably be encouraged to utilize exercise as a means towards proficiency in some sports skills, rather than exercising merely as a way of inducing muscular hypertrophy for cosmetic reasons.

The male body builder is usually compensating for inferior feelings about his maleness. By building large muscles, he seems to be saying that indeed he is a male animal, for who could expect a female to achieve such muscular development!

Corollary 12.4   Obese individuals tend to avoid physical, vigorous activity, are withdrawn socially, or evidence overcompensating social effusiveness.

Depending upon the degree of obesity, the individual who is markedly overweight is less flexible muscularly, and is inferior in quick forceful acts, particularly those which require that he move or support his body through the use of his upper limbs (20).

It is a common finding that individuals who exceed norms for height, weight, or similar qualities evidence varying degrees of feelings of inferiority. The same is true of the obese. Psychiatric literature suggests that overeating may be a form of self-punishment, and fat children are sometimes the result of overfeeding by hostile mothers.

In any case, the sensitive coach or physical educator should not provide a situation in which further punishment is heaped upon the obese. An individual who is determined to do so can out-eat any exercise program, no matter what its intensity. It would seem that the most productive approach would be to combine psychological counseling with moderate exercise in an effort to modify the fat child's physique.

That obese individuals avoid physical activity is noted daily by every physical educator throughout the country. It is painful and stressful simply to support an excess of weight; in addition, vigorous activity is more than many fat people can be expected to endure. It is suggested that an attempt to understand the reasons behind overeating is an approach superior to simply punishing the fat individual with physical exercise administered in large doses.

Summary

Relationships among physique, personality, and performance are not simple. Subtle social influences alter any attempt at outlining simple relationships among athletic participation, extroversion, sociality, hostility, and other personality traits. The statement that athletic participation enhances desirable personality traits simply cannot be supported by the available evidence. Indeed, the findings of investigations comparing the moral-ethical values of university athletes to the same values held by non-athletes have proved devastating to the coaching fraternity.

It is more reasonable to state that physical educators might aid in producing a sound personality structure in boys and early adolescents by creating situations in which they are not socially punished for ineptitude, and in which attempts are carried out to bring all boys to levels of proficiency acceptable to their peers.

Movement characteristics, gesture patterns, and ability to score touchdowns constitute a portion of the human personality. To suggest that they represent the complete behavior complex, however, seems to ignore the roles of verbal behavior and silent thought, which are important in the integration of the person to his environment.

It is apparent, from the foregoing, that personal preferences mold performance in a number of physical education activities. The individual's inclination to utilize force, various amounts of speed, and space when engaged in motoric activities must be considered by those attempting to mold his performance. Failure to start with a consideration of these personal equations in movement probably impedes more structured actions.

An individual, as he performs, constantly judges himself and is judged by others. Thus, to a large degree, an individual's physique is utilized by others as a way of ascertaining performance potential. It is therefore not surprising to find moderate correlations between physique and personality. Although some experimenters may have overstated these relationships, individuals usually behave as they perceive themselves capable of behaving, taking into consideration the physique and mental equipment with which they are endowed. A close look at the manner in which self-estimates influence potential performance is found in Chapter 3.

BIBLIOGRAPHY

1. Ahrens, Shirley. Spatial dimensions of movement. Unpublished M.A. thesis, University of California, Los Angeles, Department of Physical Education, 1966.

2. Barker, R. G. *Adjustment to physical handicap and illness.* New York: Social Science Research Council, 1953.

3. Bartley, S. Howard. *Principles of perception.* New York: Harper & Row, 1958.

4. Cortes, John B., and Gatti, Florence M. Physique and self-description of temperament. *J. Consult. Psychol.,* 1965, 29, 432–439.

5. Cratty, Bryant J. Characteristics of human learning in a locomotor maze. *Calif. J. Ed. Res.,* 1962, 14, 36–42.

6. Cratty, Bryant J. Comparisons of verbal-motor performance and learning in serial memory tasks. *Res. Quart.,* 1964, 34, 431–439.

7. Cratty, Bryant, J., and Eachus, T. Correlates of personality and motor performance in two maze tasks. Paper presented to National College Physical Education Assn., Kansas City, Kansas, 1961.

8. Cratty, Bryant J., and Williams, Harriet S. The accuracy of facing movements performed without vision. *Percept. and Mot. Skills,* 1966, 23, 1231–1238.

9. Darwin, Charles R. *The expression of emotions in animals and man.* New York: Appleton, 1872.

10. Harlow, Robert G. Masculine inadequacy and compensatory development of physique. *J. Personal.,* 1951, 19, 312–323.

11. Jones, H. E. Motor performance and growth. Berkeley: University of California Press, 1949.

12. Jones, Mary E., and Bayley, Nancy. Physical maturing among boys as related to behavior. *J. of Educ. Psychol.,* 1950, 41, 129–148.

13. Kane, John E. Psychological correlates of physique and physical abilities, in *International research in sport and physical education*, E. Jokl and E. Simon (eds.). Springfield, Illinois: Charles C. Thomas, 1964, 85–94.

14. Kline, L. W., and Johannsen, D. E. Comparative role of the face and face-body-hands as aids in identifying emotions. *J. Abnorm. and Soc. Psychol.*, 1935, 29, 415–426.

15. MacArthur, R. S. An experimental investigation of persistence and its measurement at the secondary school level. Unpublished doctoral dissertation, University of London Library, 1951.

16. Rimoldi, H. J. Personal tempo. *J. Abnorm. and Soc. Psychol.*, 1951, 46, 283–303.

17. Rosenberg, B. G., and Sutton-Smith, B. The measurement of masculinity and femininity in children; an extension and revalidation. *J. Genet. Psychol.*, 1963, 104, 259–264.

18. Sheldon, W. H., and Stevens, S. S. *The varieties of temperament*. New York: Harper & Row, 1942.

19. Walker, Richard N. Measuring masculinity and femininity by children's games choices. *Child Develop.*, 1964, 35, 961–971.

20. Weatherly, Donald. Self-perceived rate of physical maturation and personality in late adolescence. *Child Develop.*, 1964, 35, 1197–1210.

21. Werner, Alfred C., and Gottheil, Edward. Personality development and participation in college athletics. *Res. Quart.*, 1966, 37, 126–131.

In Chapter 2 attention was paid to certain personality traits as they influence performance. This chapter is intended to explore, in some detail, a component of the personality which is perhaps more influential of performance than the traits previously considered. To a marked degree, an individual's motivational level and thus performance achieved are influenced by how well he *thinks* he might do when attempting a task. Unlike some of the personality variables considered on the previous pages, the individual's aspiration level is amenable to reasonably exact experimental treatment. During the past four decades, several studies have been carried out exploring the influence of individual and group aspiration upon performance and learning of motor skills (3, 4, 18, 19).

These investigations usually involve comparisons between an individual's estimation of his performance and his actual performance. The scores obtained reflected fluctuations in estimations due to failure as well as to success. In the majority of the investigations on this subject, motor skills have been utilized. Several have used experimental tasks familiar to the physical educator, such as football playing time and grip strength (3, 19). The results of these investigations, it is believed, have important implications for the coach and physical educator. These findings are explored on the pages which follow.

Aspiration level is a component of the individual's "self" concept, and may be defined as the feeling a

3 Aspiration

person has concerning his potential for performance. It is related to the personality trait sometimes labeled *need for achievement,* to self-confidence, and to the total feelings an individual has about his capacity for intellectual as well as motor functioning (15).

13.0 *An individual's feelings about personal success are dependent primarily upon the extent to which he feels he has reached some aspired goal, not upon an absolute score obtained* (15).

Corollary 13.1   When performing motor skills, an individual invariably compares his performance score against norms he perceives are typical of individuals similar to him in age, sex, and experience (14).

Implications. Cognizance of the above statement and corollary should encourage the physical educator to attempt to define success in exact operational terms to groups of students prior to competition, i.e., is it reasonable to expect to win, or simply to perform at certain levels? The setting of feasible expectations of individual and group performance would seem a desirable undertaking for the physical educator-coach. Such estimations should not be too high for realistic achievement, and, at the same time should be high enough to encourage qualitative group and individual effort. Children and adolescents are constantly goal-setting, and shifting their expectations because of long-term and short-term experiences. Difficulty is often encountered by children who lack an extensive background of participation as they attempt to establish reasonable goals for themselves. Aiding children and adolescents to formulate reasonable expectations for their mental and physical performance, it would seem, might bolster and contribute to a sounder self-image, thus helping them to mature in desirable ways.

14.0 *Aspiration level is influenced to a marked degree by past experience* (5, 7).

Corollary 14.1   Successful past experiences will tend to raise an individual's aspiration level, while past failures will tend to lower aspirations (8, 9).
Corollary 14.2   People with high aspiration perform best (17).

Generally, past success will tend to make an individual less likely to lower aspiration upon encountering momentary failure, while past failures will make an individual more likely to lower his future performance when encountering failure. Goal setting seems to be influenced greatly by past experiences in similar tasks, the attitude toward the present task, and the feelings the individual has about personal success and failure.

Corollary 14.3   If past success has been experienced, an individual will tend to keep self-estimates high for a period of time during which failure may be encountered (13).

Implications.   The above corollaries imply that people's feelings about their performance influence performance to a marked degree. To encourage better estimates and thus better performance as a task is engaged in, or a similar type of task is engaged in, the instructor should provide initial experiences which are possible of achievement. If a difficult gymnastic stunt is to be taught, it should be properly placed in the lesson after several hours of instruction during which simple, achievable stunts are presented to the students. If initial failure is encountered, especially by the immature, further striving can be negatively influenced, and later achievement may be stunted.

Both reasonable goal-setting and an enhancement of an individual's or group's self-concept should contribute positively to striving toward successful performance when difficulty is encountered. Shifts in aspiration level and in levels of striving may be shown to be influenced to a marked degree by experimental or real life failure stress.

15.0   *Individuals upon whom pressure for achievement is placed tend to fluctuate more markedly in their voiced estimates of performance potential. These individuals react to failure immediately by lowering estimation and, at the same time, overreact to success by raising estimations too high.*

Corollary 15.1   Men are less stable in self-estimations of performance than are women (20).

Corollary 15.2   Children are less stable in self-estimations than adults (21).

Corollary 15.3   Individuals in lower economic groups are more variable in their estimations of future success than are members of higher economic groups (13).

Corollary 15.4   Less secure individuals have been found to fluctuate more in self-estimations when confronted with failure and success than are secure, well-adjusted people (7, 11).

Implications.   The above corollaries suggest that personal security is partly reflected in the manner in which people voice their expectations of performance success. The teacher should be as sensitive to overcompensatory self-estimates as to the boy or girl who takes a defeatist attitude. These individuals may be exhibiting a personality disturbance of some type, or perhaps are only immature in their outlook. In any case, aiding these people to achieve a realistic approach to their potential to perform should not only raise their level of performance, but also help them to fluctuate less in performance when momentary setbacks are encountered.

The personally insecure athlete is the one more likely to "fall apart" under the stress of competition, and to react poorly to losing as well as to winning. He will tend to engage in overcompensatory boasting following a win, and to take a negative and sullen attitude after a loss is incurred. Helping such individuals to put athletic successes and failures within a proper context should be the job of the coach and physical educator.

At the same time, if these insecure individuals are placed in positions of responsibility, e.g., as team captains, their marked fluctuations in aspiration under stress conditions could result in detrimental effects upon the team as a whole.

> **16.0**   Groups set goals just as individuals do. In general, the aspirations of groups are influenced in the same way as is goal-setting by individuals (6).

The coach-teacher should be sensitive to long-term and momentary fluctuations which can be detected in the goal-setting of various groups with which he comes in contact. The team which experiences early season losses probably needs more attention to "group self-confidence" than does a team which wins during the initial part of the season. A winning team may, of course, set unrealistically high goals initially, and even become insensitive to their own shortcomings, with disastrous results.

> **17.0**   The unique characteristics of the task influence aspiration level.

Corollary 17.1   Children tend to be less accurate when estimating scores on motor tasks than on problems involving more thought than movement (2).
Corollary 17.2   Tasks which have known performance limits, e.g., a bullseye in archery, will be more likely to produce feelings of failure when projected goals are not achieved (1, 9).

The literature supports the assumption that performance in motor tasks in which exact limits are obvious tends to be more marked by fluctuation in aspiration level when failure or success are encountered. The precision with which individuals are able to gain knowledge of their performance is influential of the exactitude with which they set future goals. For this reason, many of the experimental problems have had norms which could be manipulated by the experimenter.

Implications. Oversensitivity to failure of exactly scorable motor tasks suggests that the results of initial practice in difficult tasks should perhaps be withheld from immature performers until some basis for a sound self-estimate may be established by them. Competition introduced too early in the teaching of motor skills may have the same undesirable result for a similar reason. Competition usually requires that there be a winner and a loser, a situation which gives perhaps too exact information relative to success or failure during the initial stages of learning.

The high value children place upon successful performance in motor tasks is also implied in Corollary 17.1. Further discussion of the influence of success and failure on children's estimations of performance is found in Chapter 5.

18.0 *Various sub-cultures influence aspiration levels set by individuals.*

Corollary 18.1 When the status of an individual is challenged, as when competing against individuals perceived by him as lower in status, the more he is likely to either over- or underestimate performance (13).

Corollary 18.2 The aspiration levels of parents have been demonstrated to be related to the aspiration level of their children (16, 17).

Corollary 18.3 "Self-reliance training" on the part of parents may result in high needs for achievement by their children (17).

Implications. The statements above suggest that, while the physical educator-coach may to some extent manipulate the goal-setting and general motivational level of the children in his charge, a number of other social influences also mold their feelings about success and failure. It is unclear how various parts of the child's sub-culture specifically influence his performance, i.e., to generally achieve in everything he attempts, or only in specified activities? In any case, sensitivity to the influence of parents, peers, and other societal groups upon the aspiration levels of children and youth might prompt the coach or teacher to hold parent conferences, and to discuss a child's performance to secure a higher level of striving.

It is believed that teacher-child communication will be enhanced and tension alleviated when the former is more cognizant of the importance of outside influences upon the level of achievement with which the student is satisfied. For a coach or physical education instructor to overcome the negative influences of parents and peer groups upon the performance aspirations of an individual youth is often a difficult undertaking.

The teacher-educator should aid an individual boy being subjected to various pressures for success by components of his sub-culture to place such pressures in perspective. For example, the coaches of the age-group swimming team will many times become aware of the "too interested" parent who is pressuring a child unduly for achievement, and may actually be impeding his performance by doing so. Parent-child-coach conferences should aid in helping this kind of situation, and result in a more positive attitude being taken by both parent and child, which will ultimately result in better performance by the latter.

19.0   *Aspiration level is both specific and general (5, 8, 12).*

Corollary 19.1   Individuals who achieve in classrooms at high levels despite ordinary intellectual endowments can be expected to perform well in motor skills (18).

Corollary 19.2   If the tasks compared are significantly different in nature, aspiration level will usually shift.

Corollary 19.3   If motor tasks are similar, the level of aspiration an individual evidences when performing one will usually be predictable of the level of success he sets for himself prior to attempting the second.

Implications. Aspiration levels in gross motor skills are significantly different in late adolescents from their aspirations in fine motor skills. Argument for the generality of aspiration level, i.e., that it is predictable from classroom performance to motor activity, suggests that there is an underlying level of "striving" unique to each individual. Although there is little research supporting this idea, perhaps levels of aspiration in classrooms might be significantly affected in a positive way by providing experiences in which achievement is realized in sports activities. The influence of motor skill success upon classroom striving or lack of motivation should be expected to be particularly marked on the part of boys in childhood and early adolescence. A large portion of their self-concept at this age hinges upon their success in physical activities highly valued by their peers. Thus, success or failure in this component of their behavior might be expected to significantly alter their total self-concept.

The literature on transfer indicates that, for positive transfer to occur, it must be deliberately sought. If the teacher or coach finds a boy whose aspirations are channelized only toward success in sports activity, he might be encouraged to generalize his feelings of mastery to other kinds of endeavors. Although society provides rewards early in life for masculine success in athletic endeavors, later success is in most cases more dependent upon other kinds of behavior. It is believed that the coach and physical education instructor might bring a more mature perspective to the child's value system by pointing out to him that his needs for achievement might be gradually shifted to include not only success on the athletic field, but also might encompass successful performance in tasks involving thought.

In general, an individual's goal-setting reflects an attempt to avoid failure, to exceed past performance levels, and to maintain a positive self-image. The stability and consistencies of his past experiences, as well as the consistency of his own personality, are reflected in fluctuations in his goal-setting behavior.

Aspiration level is intimately connected with the social context. The individual is constantly comparing his performance with social expectations for one of his age and ability. When comparing himself with norms he must conceive of some peer group with which he identifies. One's feeling about his past performance is a decided influence, not only upon his feelings about future performance, but upon absolute performance levels reached. The coach or physical education teacher who ignores this important variable when dealing with children and youth does so at his peril.

BIBLIOGRAPHY

1. Allport, F. H. Influence of group upon association and thought. *J. Exp. Psychol.*, 1920, 3, 159–182.

2. Anderson, Harold H., and Brandt, H. F. Study of motivation involving self announced goals of fifth grade children of the concept of level of aspiration. *J. Soc. Psychol.*, 1939, 10, 209–232.

3. Clark, H. H., and Clark, D. H. Relationships between levels of aspiration and selected physical factors of boys aged nine years. *Res. Quart.*, 1961, 32, 12–19.

4. Clark, H. H., and Stratton, Stephen. A level of aspiration test based on the grip strength efforts of nine-year-old boys. *Child Dev.*, 1962, 33, 897–905.

5. Cratty, Bryant J. *Social dimensions of physical activity.* Englewood Cliffs, New Jersey: Prentice-Hall, Inc., 1967, Chap. III, Aspiration level.

6. Ex, J. The nature of contact between cooperating persons and their expectancy concerning the level of their common achievement. *Acta Psychol.*, 1959, 16, 99–107.

7. Eysenck, H. J. (ed.). *Handbook of abnormal psychology.* New York: Basic Books, Inc., 1961, 284–291.

8. Frank, Jerome D. Recent studies of the level of aspiration. *Psychol. Bull.*, 1941, 38, 218–226.

9. Frank, Jerome D. Some psychological determinants of the level of aspiration. *Am. J. Psychol.*, 1937, 45, 285–293.

10. Gardner, John W. Level of aspiration. *J. Exp. Psychol.*, 1939, 25, 601–621.

11. Gardner, John W. The relation of certain personality variables to level of aspiration. *J. Psychol.*, 1940, 9, 191–206.

12. Gould, Rosalind. An experimental analysis of "level of aspiration." *Genet. Psychol. Monog.*, 1939, 21, 1–115.

13. Gould, Rosalind. Some sociological determinants of goal striving. *J. Soc. Psychol.*, 1961, 13, 461–473.

14. Gruen, E. W. Level of aspiration in relation to personality factors in adolescents. *Child Dev.*, 1945, 16, 181–188.

15. Hoppe, F. Erfolg und Misserfolg. *Psych. Forsch.*, 1930, 14, 1–62.

16. Little, Sue W., and Cohen, L. D. Goal setting behavior of asthmatic children and of their mothers for them. *J. Personal.*, 1950, 19, 376–389.

17. Rosen, Bernard D., and D'Andrade, Roy. The psychosocial origins of achievement motivation. *Sociometry*, 1959, 22, 185–218.

18. Ryan, Dean E. Competitive performance in relation to achievement motivation and anxiety. Paper presented to National Convention of Am. Assn. for Health, Physical Education, and Recreation. Minneapolis, Minnesota, 1963.

19. Smith, C. H. Influence of athletic success and failure on the level of aspiration. *Res. Quart.*, 1949, 20, 196.

20. Sumner, F. C., and Johnson, E. E. Sex differences in levels of aspiration and in self-estimates of performance in a classroom situation. *J. Psychol.*, 1949, 27, 483–490.

21. Walter L. M., and Marzole, S. S. The relation of sex, age, and school achievement to levels of aspiration. *J. of Ed. Psychol.*, 1951, 42, 285–292.

part two

MATURATION

A discussion of perceptual-motor behavior as a function of maturation can have either a psychological or physiological orientation. As the focus of the text is upon psychological findings, the material within this chapter will not offer an analysis of the manner in which various biochemical and anatomical factors influence behavior as people age. It is not intended, however, to negate the basic importance of various hormonal and structural fluctuations which influence movement characteristics in childhood and adolescence.

The statements which follow emphasize what people *do,* and not the neurological, biochemical, and anatomical reasons *why* they do them. Even with this limitation, they represent only a cursory look at the perceptual-motor behavior of people as they mature. Maturation is a continual process beginning at gestation and ending with death; a process marked by increased complexity of functioning on the part of the individual and by the gradual molding of behavior through experience. Thus, the initial principles, concerning infancy and childhood, are perhaps more valid, while the later ones are less definite and dependent upon more complex variables and the possibility of a multitude of experiences. In any case, it is believed that the statement and corollaries presented on the pages to follow may provide a springboard from which fruitful discussions may be launched. Detailed descriptive information may be located in some of the texts listed at the conclusion of each chapter within this part.

4 Perceptual-Motor Behavior in Infancy, Childhood, Adolescence, Adulthood and by the Aged

This chapter deals with analyses of the performance of the child, the adolescent, the adult, and the aged acting alone. Chapter 5 presents principles applicable to the performance of infants, children, and adolescents in groups, while Chapter 6 presents principles which relate to the influence of an important sub-group upon the performance attributes of children—their family.

> **20.0**   *Initial movements of the infant are largely involuntary and reflexive in nature* (18).

Corollary 20.1   Rather early in life, visual-motor integration occurs, the eyes see the hands move, and, in turn, their movement begins to be placed under voluntary control (12).

Corollary 20.2   During the first few weeks of life, the infant engages in fixating and then in tracking behavior with the visual system (12).

Implications. There is sufficient evidence which suggests that the infant not only has an early capacity to perceive his own and others' movements, but that permitting him increased opportunity to do so has a marked influence upon his later perceptual-motor attributes. Many pediatricians will, for example, suggest various complex and colored patterns be placed where the infant, in his crib, may observe them. Likewise, it is sometimes suggested that the infant be left free to observe the clenchings of his fists and the movements of his legs in order to hasten desirable visual-motor development.

There is a reasonable amount of clinical and experimental evidence to support the contention that early movement experiences on the part of the infant, i.e., the tactile and playful interactions between parent and infant, can positively influence the child's movement characteristics later in life. Recent experimental evidence indicates that the child's movements prior to birth are positively related to his later movement attributes. Children who were noted to have engaged in more extensive movements prior to birth evidenced more advanced motor development as infants and young children than did children who did not engage in pre-birth movements of as long a duration.

> **21.0**   *Many of these early reflexes come under the domination of voluntary control, while others persist and mold voluntary perceptual-motor behaviors* (18).

Corollary 21.1   The prehensile reflex (the strong grasp at birth) gradually disappears, and voluntary manipulative behavior begins to emerge in its place (17).

Corollary 21.2   The locomotor, cross-extension reflex similarly comes under voluntary control, although it continues to support correct crawling and walking patterns later in infancy and throughout life (19).

Implications. Inappropriate interactions between various reflexes and voluntary movements during early infancy and childhood are often indicative of some kind of basic neuromotor abnormality. The mother and the nursery school teacher should be sensitive to inappropriate posturings on the part of children. It is through careful observation of a child's neuromotor patterns, specifically crawling behavior, prehension-manipulative activities, and arm-leg integration in throwing, walking, running, and similar acts, that initially provides the cues that "something is wrong" with the child. This early perceptual-motor malfunctioning, if not modified by early training, might prove harder to correct later in childhood. The close relationship between perceptual-motor problems and later learning problems in the classroom, primarily those evidenced as the child attempts to organize words and letters in words and makes his first efforts to write, has been alluded to by several prominent child development experts within recent years.

22.0   *The assumption of voluntary control of the larger muscles of the trunk and upper body precedes gaining control over smaller muscles and movements of the lower body (18).*

Programs of movement activities for infants and young children should be composed initially of activities to enhance the control and integration of the larger muscle groups of the body. They should start with tasks involving trunk muscles, e.g., rolling and turning movements, and then progress to integrations of the limbs. At the final stages in such programs, activities intended to enhance fine muscle control should be incorporated.

Tasks to heighten balance, agility, and tumbling movements, as well as basic locomotor activities, should form the basis for programs of physical education for pre-school and primary school youngsters. In the upper primary school grades, more practice in activities involving complex perceptual judgments should be included.

Corollary 22.1   Characteristics of locomotor activity seem more inherent than manipulative capacities and activities involving the upper limbs (4).

Implications. It is a commonly advanced principle that programs for young children should emphasize activities which enhance the control of larger muscle groups and basic capacities rather than such complex perceptual-motor activities as ball catching or fine manipulation. There are indications that the child, rather than developing in a neat series of steps, as some would have us believe, actually progresses in a series of spirals, advancing forward in several kinds of capacities at the same time while, at other times, retrogressing.

Although a child must walk before running and must balance on one foot before jumping on it and learning to skip, the assumption that basic locomotor capacities influence and must precede classroom training does not seem substantiated by the current experimental literature. Visual tracking usually precedes crawling and creeping, and so activities which encourage visual-motor integrations, such as the tracking of balls hung on strings, should accompany activities which seek to enhance the child's control over his large muscles in balance tasks or agility exercises.

> **23.0**   *Prior to the age of two, physical ability is difficult to separate from social, intellectual, and verbal behavior.*

Corollary 23.1   Verbal ability is often developed in response to movements; "come here," "give me that," "no . . no," or "stop doing something" constitute the initial verbal cues to which the infant is exposed (7).

Recent investigations demonstrate the facilitating manner in which games may be utilized to teach verbal concepts to children of elementary school age. The parts of speech, components of sentences, and similar concepts can be incorporated into games for children of all ages with demonstrable positive influence upon the learning process.

Corollary 23.2   Social behavior during infancy has been assessed by noting, for the most part, attributes which are primarily motor in nature (2, 5, 7).

Social behavior and motor behavior of infants are inseparable. If a child is socially outgoing, it implies in part that he can move from place to place effectively. Social interactions between children partially depend upon their ability to manipulate play materials, and to engage in games. Enhancing the sociality of young children can be accomplished through the media of games of a vigorous as well as of a passive nature.

Corollary 23.3   Non-verbal measures of I.Q. administered during the early years of life primarily involve perceptual-motor functioning, the placing of patterns in the proper holes, and so on (7).

Some have suggested that abstract thought does not occur prior to the development of verbal behavior, and motoric behavior precedes verbal behavior. In the absence of complex verbal behavior, intellectual functioning *must* be assessed by noting what the child can do with his visual-motor action systems.

Implications. This does not mean that movement forms the basis for all cognitive functioning. It does, however, imply that faulty early perceptual-motor development can limit the opportunities the child has to explore and to learn about himself and objects in his environment, and can seriously limit his growing intellectual awareness. Numerous clinical studies of the motorically handicapped attest to the importance of manipulative behavior to learning. Child development experts observing the normal child usually suggest the importance of an early "sensory-motor" period in the intellectual growth of the child.

Games for children should not always merely lead toward vigorous activity for its own sake. Activities in which children are encouraged to think, plan, and control their actions are also of considerable worth. There are relatively few classroom concepts which cannot be taught and explored through movement activities on the part of children.

> **24.0**   With increasing age, the infant and child evidence more specificity of skill; the identification of general coordination by assessing performance on a few basic tasks becomes more difficult.

Performance in perceptual-motor skills early in infancy seems more dependent upon inherent neuromotor characteristics, while in later years it is more dependent upon specific environmental experience, i.e., learning. This implies that, during the early months of life, assessments of neuro-motor problems and deficiencies may be easier. Later in life, the abilities of the infant and the child may be largely due to experiences provided in his environment, thus making an accurate over-all assessment of basic characteristics a somewhat tenuous undertaking.

Corollary 24.1   Sex differences in general movement characteristics and performance scores become discernible at a relatively early age—from two to three years (13).

Corollary 24.2   Hand preference begins to be identifiable about the third or fourth month of life in many cases, although this is not usually well established until about the sixth year of life (17).

Corollary 24.3   Body build begins to exert an influence upon performance by the nursery school years, i.e., two and three years of age (20).

Corollary 24.4   Individual differences in level of vigorous activity participated in begin to manifest themselves by the age of three (20). Even during these early years, boys are noted to move more vigorously than girls.

Implications. This rather early specialization in the movement attributes of infants and children indicates that environment can exert an important influence over their behavior. Construction of a proper play environment containing apparatus for climbing, opportunities for rolling and handling objects, as well as providing the impetus for vigorous running, should significantly influence the developmental pattern of individuals in early childhood. Failure to provide opportunities for vigorous movement in the absence of social approval by parents and interested adults has been demonstrated to alter significantly behavior in adolescence and early adulthood.

The increasing specificity of perceptual-motor functioning of children suggests that the range of activities offered should be broad, and include tasks which encourage balancing, agility, locomotor activities, and hand-eye and body-eye coordinations, as well as games which encourage visual tracking of objects. It is believed essential, however, to first provide basic experiences which enable the child to gain mastery over his own body, involving locating body parts and relating his body to other objects in his environment. Then he should be confronted with activities which require that complex judgments be made relative to balls in space, and requiring the use of extensions of the body (rackets, bats) to intercept them. Many testing programs involving analyses of the performance of children in early childhood indicate that girls are more agile than boys, because of the emphasis upon such agility-producing activities as hop-scotch, while boys become more proficient in ball handling skills. It should be emphasized that the child throws and catches balls with his total body, not just with his eyes and hands. Failure to provide basic agility and balance experiences may impede the acquisition of more complex perceptual attributes necessary in many ball games.

There is a considerable amount of evidence attesting to the ability of children, as they mature, to profit from specific instructions when confronted with motor skills. Ball throwing and similar skills have been found to be highly improvable with the introduction of planned instruction. To simply throw a ball to children of middle primary years is to short-change them in terms of skill improvement. Instructions in the form of verbal directions, manual guidance, and visual demonstration have all been found helpful in the improvement of the perceptual-motor attributes of young children.

> **25.0** There are reasonably consistent progressions in the acquisition of several types of perceptual-motor capacities. These progressions may vary within limits, however, within an individual child (2, 11, 13).

Corollary 25.1   Locomotor behavior is relatively stratified in the stages of development through which a child passes. He rolls over, crawls, creeps, postures, walks, runs, jumps, and hops in a reasonably predictable order (2).

Children with identifiable gait problems should be aided to improve by specific practice at the level at which difficulty is evidenced. The legs form a "base" from which the child moves; if his locomotor behavior is faulty, effective throwing and agility movements required as he attempts to intercept balls become difficult, if not impossible. Extensive practice not only in the specifics of locomotion, but also in activities requiring accurate use of the legs (e.g., soccer drills) will prove effective in improving the child's abilities to move his legs well.

Corollary 25.2   Hand-eye coordination, as evidenced in drawing tasks, shows a reasonably orderly series of developmental steps (8).

Left-right movements seem easier to track, and the child can draw a line horizontally before he can track objects moving up and down or draw up-down movements on a page. Lateral movements and drawings which reflect lateral organization of hand and movement are seen later in the child's motoric repertoire.

Implications.   Sensitivity to these somewhat orderly stages of development on the part of the teacher or parent can aid in the early diagnosis of perceptual-motor problems which may be reflected in classroom learning and, at the same time, should guide individuals who attempt to provide various kinds of movement experiences for children (dance, rhythm, art work) as well as gross activities on the playground.

A child's scribblings will at first probably take the form of spirals, clockwise in the case of movements with the left hand, and counterclockwise when the right hand is involved. Later the child will begin to refine his movements and become able to make first horizontal and then vertical strokes on a page. Next lateral movements are seen, and later these various movements will be made with more accuracy as he becomes able to inscribe them within guidelines. Movements crossing the mid-line of his body are more difficult, and occur later in the developmental process than movements on one side of the body. Similarly, movements in the center of the page are usually made with more accuracy than movements at the periphery. The child should be given every encouragement to engage in this kind of activity through the presentation of finger-painting, coloring, and various drawing tasks.

A series of problems on a drawing board which are incongruent with the development of various hand-eye capacities will result in frustrations in the child. Although some recent theorists suggest that the "filling in" of developmental indices of motor maturation is crucial to the intellectual functioning of the child, experimental evidence does not support the exactitude of these statements concerning mind-body relationships.

There is extensive clinical speculation, however, that more complex perceptual-motor capacities depend upon the early acquisition of basic attributes, and that *certain components* of classroom learning, particularly those involving the manipulation of concrete problems, i.e., reading, writing, and spelling, are enhanced if the child has formed a sound basis of simpler perceptual-motor capacities from which to proceed.

26.0   *During childhood, children master a variety of complex skills rather quickly and, in general, exhibit a remarkable* *capacity to move their bodies in a variety of ways if exposed to the proper experiences* (11).

Corollary 26.1   Practice has a marked effect upon the performance of children. They gain the capacity to watch and copy movements of others and to respond to verbal directions.

Corollary 26.2   Sex differences begin to be more marked during late childhood, with the girls maintaining superiority on certain flexibility-agility measures, while the boys surpass them in tasks requiring force, speed, and power (6).

Corollary 26.3   There is an increased capacity to summate forces in movements i.e., throwing and jumping, by integrating several parts of the body at the same time in middle and late childhood (11).

Corollary 26.4   Children, when learning complex skills in which speed and accuracy are emphasized equally, first emphasize speed, then accuracy, and later effectively integrate both speed and accuracy to the appropriate degree (21).

Implications. Indications presented above suggest that programs of activities for children should be reasonably complex, and consist of activities graded in difficulty which offer challenges to a child at various stages of his development. The tendency in elementary school physical education programs to present a rather static list of games, ignoring these emerging capacities, should be examined critically.

In the upper elementary school grades, increased opportunities should be allowed to permit boys and girls to engage in separate programs of games. Although it is difficult to determine whether emerging sex differences are due to inherent or environmental factors, they exist nonetheless and should be accommodated for in the form of diverse programs of activities.

> **27.0**   *Unilateral perceptual-motor behavior is a multi-factored phenomena evidenced in hand use, eye preference, and various locomotor activities.*

Corollary 27.1   It seems helpful if a child has acquired the inclination to utilize the same arm-hand and preferred eye when engaging in perceptual-motor activities (17).

Implications. Many authorities suggest that various postural imbalances stemming from opposite hand-eye use are reflected in distortions in visual-space perception. Other writers merely suggest that it is "helpful" if a child, rather early in life, "decides" upon a hand-leg on the same side as the eye he prefers. Although the physical educator should refer children with apparent cross-dominance to the psychologist or pediatrician for further evaluation, sensitivity to improper arm-leg-eye integration should make the elementary physical education teacher a valuable assistant to the educational therapist, the psychologist, and other professional people interested in the child's welfare.

Unilateral behavior does not seem, however, to be of overriding importance for the child's cognitive-symbolic functioning, as several authors would have us believe. Various sub-humans evidenced preferred handedness about three million years ago, while possessing brains about one-third the size of the human cortex. Further elaboration of the possible relationships between laterality and intellectuality are found in Chapter 20.

Emerging unilateral hand use seems a normal part of the increased differentiation of function of the child, which finally is stabilized in a normal child at about the age of six. At that time one hand becomes the predominant one used. Leg use is not as well established, and frequently a child will change leg use depending upon the type of task he is facing.

In general, a child should be encouraged to adopt unilateral behavior in terms of limb use simply because it will produce greater skill, insofar as a single hand receives more practice time than it would if the time were split between the two upper limbs.

> **28.0** *In early and middle adolescence, a combination of social, physiological, and psychological factors converge to influence the performance of boys and girls.*

Corollary 28.1   Rather exact social roles relative to quantitative and qualitative aspects of physical activity are assigned to boys and girls during adolescence (3).

Corollary 28.2   Boys, during adolescence, are given every social sanction to do well in vigorous sports; measures of their physical capacity correlate highly with performance scores (3).

Corollary 28.3   Cultural sanctions "blunt" the performance of adolescent girls, although a trend seems to indicate that American culture is beginning to offer more encouragement to girls to participate in vigorous games. Capacity measures of adolescent girls are not highly correlated with performance scores.

Corollary 28.4   The physical performance scores of girls are at their apex at about the age of 15; in boys, physical performance tends to peak at about the age of 18 (6).

Implications. The divergent roles and capacities of girls and boys during adolescence suggest that for much of the time they should be separated when attempting to elicit optimum performance. At the same time, the girls should be given every encouragement to continue to value and participate in rather vigorous activities. There is no physiological evidence which suggests that the capacities of girls should begin to drop after their fifteenth year, and much of this performance decline must be attributed to disinclination to move vigorously, caused by negative cultural pressures and sanctions. Contrary to common belief, there is no experimental evidence that adolescents enter an "awkward age" relative to the performance of physical skills. Although tension in social situations may cause an adolescent to stumble against the furniture, available data suggest that performance capacities of adolescents reach even higher levels from ages 12 to 18.

These findings suggest that reasonably high expectations should be placed upon adolescents in a performance situation. They are generally reaching, or are at, their peak in strength, endurance, and the ability to integrate various visual-motor action systems. The primary problem, of course, is encountered in motivating girls to realize their potential and utilize their increasing capacities for movement.

In addition to physical tasks which encourage optimum performance, activities should be made available in which adolescents' masculinity and femininity may be evidenced. The girls should be given an opportunity to engage in graceful dance movements, and the boys should be exposed to combatives designed to promote wholesome male aggressiveness.

29.0   *During adulthood, basic capacities decrease while experience and opportunity for learning skills increase (20).*

Corollary 29.1   Complex skills tend to improve during adulthood, while those requiring primarily basic capacities (i.e., strength, endurance) tend to decrease in level of performance (16, 21).

Corollary 29.2   The ability to learn a motor skill does not seem to be altered during adulthood. The speed with which adults learn new skills from ages 20 to 40 remains relatively constant (1).

Implications. Perceptual-motor activities emphasized during adulthood should be primarily those in which complexity of functioning is predominant over the necessity to exhibit basic performance capacities possessed during adolescence. Although the decrease in adult capacity measures can largely be attributed to motivation, there is usually a real decline in adult abilities to exert force and otherwise function in strength-endurance activities as compared to their performances in adolescence.

Activities for adults should be those in which they may not only exhibit a moderate amount of basic ability, but should also involve an intellectual challenge. Adults prefer to utilize their background of experience to solve motor problems, rather than simply "bludgeon through" activities as they did in early and late adolescence. The adult requires careful instruction to accompany the presentation of relatively new motor activities, and if this instruction is lacking or faulty his participation will often be deferred.

Adults' preferences concerning activities are relatively fixed, which suggests the importance of exposing the growing adolescent to a variety of physical experiences. The older adult becomes increasingly reluctant to attempt learning new skills, with the chance of concomitant embarrassment. Attitudes about activities acquired early in life seem to carry over into adult activity preferences.

> **30.0** *In the aged, marked shifts occur in ability to remember and to process information related to complex skills* (20).

Tissue changes occur in the aged, muscles become less strong and flexible, and respiratory systems evidence less efficient functioning, and certain perceptual differences modify their abilities to learn new and complex motor skills. More time is needed by the aged to integrate input and output, i.e., their reaction time increases; they seek more instructions when learning a new task, and in other ways indicate that changes are occurring in their ability to process information (19).

Implications. Programs for the aged should be carefully graded, and administered by patient instructors familiar with the perceptual-motor capacities of those in their charge. Although exceptionally vigorous older citizens frequently distort the experimental findings as well as the perceptions of those operating senior citizens' programs, in general, the older member of our society usually likes to be challenged in ways not threatening to his self-image.

The older individual prefers to be led carefully into new skills, rather than exploring them on a trial and error basis as he would have preferred when younger. He does not react well to the stress of failure, as he does not wish to be confronted with objective evidence of his declining capacities. Directions regulating games will often have to be repeated, as there seems to be a loss of short-term memory ability while retention of the memory of distant events remains. The older individual requires close visual inspection of his movements, as he once did as a child when first attempting to organize his motor patterns. Careful attention to these differences in the performance and learning capacities of the aged should result in programs which will more exactly meet their needs and obtain their support.

Individuals seldom perform motor skills in isolation. Even when by themselves, they silently assess their progress or lack of it against social norms of which they are usually acutely aware. Chapter 5 discusses some of the implications which may be derived from principles obtained from observation and measurement of infants, children, and adolescents interacting and observing each other when performing motor tasks.

BIBLIOGRAPHY

1. Bachman, John C. Motor learning and performance as related to age and sex in two measures of balance coordination. *Res. Quart.*, 1961, 32, 123–137.

2. Bayley, Nancy. The development of motor abilities, during the first three years. Monographs for the Society for Research in Child Development, Washington, D.C., 1935.

3. Coleman, James S. *The adolescent society.* New York: The Free Press of Glencoe, 1961.

4. Cratty, Bryant J. A comparison of fathers and sons in physical ability. *Res. Quart.*, 1960, 31, 12–15.

5. Doll, Edgar A. A genetic scale of social maturity. *Am. J. Orthopsychiatry,* 1953, 180–188.

6. Fleishman, Edwin A. The dimensions of physical fitness—the nationwide normative and developmental study of basic tests. Technical Report No. 4, The Office of Naval Research, Department of Industrial Administration and Department of Psychology, Yale University, New Haven, Conn., August, 1962.

7. Gesell, Arnold, and Amatruda, Catherine S. *Developmental diagnosis.* New York: P. B. Hoeber, Inc., 1960.

8. Gesell, Arnold and Thompson, Helen. *Infant behavior, its genesis and growth.* New York: McGraw-Hill Book Co., Inc., 1934.

9. Goodenough, F. L. Measuring behavior traits by means of repeated short samples. *J. Juv. Res.*, 1928, 12, 230–235.

10. Goodenough, F. L. The relationship of the intelligence of pre-school children to the education of their parents. *School and Society,* 1927, 26, 54–56.

11. Goodenough, F. L., and Brian, C. R. Certain factors underlying the acquisition of motor skills by pre-school youngsters. *J. Exp. Psychol.,* 1929, 12, 127–155.

12. Haith, Marshall M. The response of the human newborn to visual movement. *J. Exp. Child Psychol.,* 1965, 3, 235–243.

13. Hicks, James Allen. The acquisition of motor skill in young children. *University of Iowa Studies in Child Welfare,* 4, No. V, University of Iowa Press, 1929.

14. Jesild, A. T., and Ding, G. F. A study of the laughing and smiling of pre-school children. *J. Genet. Psychol.,* 1932, 40, 452–472.

15. Kidd, Aline H., and Rivoire, Jeanne L. (eds.). *Perceptual development in children.* New York: International Universities Press, Inc., 1966.

16. Miles, W. R. Age and human ability. *Psychol. Review.,* 1933, 40, 90–123.

17. Palmer, Robert D. Development of a differentiated handedness. *Psychol. Bull.*, 1964, 62, 257–272.

18. Peiper, Albrecht. *Cerebral function of infancy and childhood.* Leipzig, Germany: VEB Georg Thieme, 1961.

19. Singleton, W. T. The change of movement timing with age. *Brit. J. Psychol.*, 1954, 65, 166–172.

20. Walker, Richard N. Body-build and behavior in young children. Body-build and nursery school teacher's ratings. *Monograph of the Society for Research in Child Development,* Gesell Institute of Child Development, 1952, 3, 27, 84.

21. Welford, A. T. *Aging and human skill.* New York: Oxford University Press, 1958.

22. Williams, Harriet. Perception of the pathway of missiles by elementary school children. Unpublished study, Perceptual-Motor Learning Laboratory, University of California, Los Angeles, 1966.

As the child matures, he becomes increasingly aware of and responsive to his social surroundings. Initially, his responses are molded by the smiling faces of his mother and father; later, his perceptual-motor behavior becomes influenced directly and indirectly by other children with whom he comes in contact. Infants, children, and adolescents affect each other subtly through the relatively unconscious pick-up of gestures, and through direct and obvious attempts to influence one another.

At first, the presence of an onlooker generally excites the young child, and relatively little measurable performance change is evidenced. Later, the child's performance begins to be influenced in rather exact ways when he is being watched. The statements which follow represent summaries of a survey of the literature concerning the influence of competition and cooperation, various leadership patterns, and onlookers upon the performance of infants, children, and adolescents. Other basic principles of group interaction are found in Part VI.

> **31.0**   *The complexity of the social interaction of infants and children gradually increases in a reasonably predictable sequence (4, 5, 25).*

Corollary 31.1   Infant-child play progresses from solitary to imitative-parallel play, through same-sex pairings, to small group interactions, and finally to complex team situations with codified rules (5, 25).

5 Maturation and Performance in Groups

Frequently atypical emotional, intellectual, and social development will manifest itself in social patterns of play which are too infantile for a child of a given chronological age. A child of six or seven who seems only to engage in solitary or imitative play, for example, should be some cause for concern. On the other hand, a child who seems to be acquiring the ability to relate effectively to others in groups of increasing size and complexity is exhibiting a "normal" pattern of social development.

Implications. Designing games for children which require social interaction in advance of the child's normal capacities for one of his years is fraught with disaster. Initially the child seems only able to relate to one other individual, and this relationship is often not obvious or direct. Prior to the age of two, a child seems capable only of relating to one other child at a time, and will usually copy the friend's activities without any direct social contact. Later, a child plays in an obvious way with another child or with a parent. The boys, perhaps because of cultural expectations, progress more rapidly to the stage of interaction which requires exact rules. Young girls usually prefer to play in less structured situations.

Maturational lags may be readily identified by the sensitive teacher when observing the maximum capacity a child seems to possess relative to the complexity of social interactions. While it is usual for a very bright child to engage sometimes in solitary observation even when in the presence of others, it is also usual for such a child, at times, to relate to one or more of his peers. Inability to do so usually indicates some kind of adjustment problem and/or maturational lag.

Corollary 31.2 The bright, active child prefers to play with older peers, whereas the dull, inactive child prefers to play with younger peers (2, 7).

Implications. Designing programs for children based solely upon chronological age is a dangerous undertaking. Programs based upon a child's capacities for group interaction of varying degrees of complexity seem a more sound approach. The degree of complexity a child can handle in social relations with his peers is generally predictive of his general social adjustment, intelligence, and capacity for handling, remembering, and integrating complex information. Exceeding a child's capacity for complex social interactions when carrying out a program of physical activity is unsound, to say the least.

The sensitive teacher will provide groups in which an effective mixture of children is combined, so that those somewhat withdrawn are brought out by the socially more active individuals. Placing children into groups composed solely of children with similar perceptual-motor, emotional, and/or gender identification problems can be as harmful as leaving such children in larger groups whose insensitive members may transmit social punishment because of their ineptitudes.

32.0   Slight, positive correlations are usually obtained when comparing the social attributes of children to their physical skills (15, 29).

Corollary 32.1   Children who are most liked are either average or above average in physical ability.

Corollary 32.2   Social behavior of young children has been evaluated primarily through observation of various gross and fine motor skills (10).

Implications. Children judge each other primarily upon the basis of what they can *do*. The society of the child is not composed of subtle innuendoes, but of direct and observable behavior. A child who cannot or is unwilling to engage in gross physical output is not generally accorded as high a place in the status hierarchy as is a child who participates vigorously in the available games and activities. All teachers observing the play activities of children should be sensitive to the children who *cannot* or *do not* act, and should attempt to ascertain the reason for their reluctance. The teacher should attempt to provide situations in which innumerable activities are available so that all children can participate. Specific instruction in skills should be given the inept performers. Some children seem able to copy the throwing patterns and other appropriate skills from their more successful peers, while others cannot. The teacher should provide appropriate instruction periods for the latter individuals.

33.0   Young children performing in front of one or more onlookers evidence general patterns of excitation which are seldom translated into performance improvement (23).

Corollary 33.1   Children below six years of age do not tend to persist in endurance tasks in the presence of others. The presence of a "liked" peer tends to distract, and hence disrupt coordinated performance; the presence of a "disliked" peer results in performance improvement because of the lack of distraction (16, 23).

Corollary 33.2   General excitability of children of five negatively affects throwing accuracy (23).

Corollary 33.3   Boys over the age of six are more positively influenced by an audience when performing than are girls (23).

Implications. Pressure in the presence of spectators, particularly close friends, is probably best omitted when working on skill improvement in children until they reach the age of six or seven. Even improvement in endurance and strength tasks is not evidenced, as is usually the case later in life, when children under six perform in front of an audience.

At the age of six children seem to undergo a transformation concerning their feelings about themselves in a social context. They attempt to excel in direct and positive ways after six, and generally increase the level of performance when others are watching. Before that age, the presence of others can often prove disruptive of measurable strength-endurance tasks and, at times, of skilled acts.

Extremely young children (two to three years) become aware of various cultural pressures to do well, in the form of parental expectations and peer pressures. However, their ability to change intensity or accuracy of their perceptual-motor behavior effectively in response to this cultural pressure remains behind their ability to simply become aware of it.

It would seem that the best activities to utilize with children below six are those in which there is little demand for optimum performance, and in which a child can relax and perform relatively unencumbered by social pressures. Children can be encouraged to develop individually during these years, even in the presence of others, through the use of rhythmics and similar activities which encourage a variety of movements without the concomitant pressure to reach optimum performance levels.

> **34.0**   There are detectable trends in the assumption of competitive and cooperative behavior on the part of young children. Competition precedes cooperation (14).

Corollary 34.1   Competition appears during the end of the first year of life, whereas cooperative behavior in small groups does not appear until about the fifth year (14).

Corollary 34.2   Competition occurs when two or more children both desire the same goal or object and perceive their chances to achieve this are reasonably good (14).

Corollary 34.3   Competition will occur between two children when they perceive their abilities to be nearly alike.

Babies will compete for an object more *vigorously* if they are within three months of each other's age. Identical twins will compete more than will fraternal twins or siblings (6, 14).

Implications. Competition in children can have desirable and undesirable consequences. In general, competition raises a child's tension level so that, under competitive circumstances, improvement will many times be noted in simple forceful acts or endurance activities. On the other hand, increased tension levels will disrupt skilled coordinations. To exploit competitive urges among children successfully, the instructor should evaluate carefully the type of task in which improvement is desired as well as a child's perceptions of his own capabilities in relation to the capacities of those with whom he is competing.

In order to encourage successful competition between pairs or groups of children who do not perceive themselves alike in ability, teachers should handicap one of the individuals or groups in order to engender mutual striving. If the two groups of individuals do not view each other as reasonably close in ability, competitive behavior will usually not occur.

Although such handicapping will sometimes be accurately perceived by the competing children, the reasons for it might be explained in order to avoid stress and confusion in the participants. One child may be started ahead of others in a race, or perhaps be placed further from a target when throwing for accuracy. There are innumerable means through which the sensitive teacher can encourage competitive behavior in situations in which it is not likely to occur because of perceived differences in ability.

> **35.0**   *There are marked sex differences relative to the social importance of physical activity which are evidenced rather early in childhood.*

Corollary 35.1   Boys perform better in the presence of a peer onlooker, after the age of six, than do girls (23).

Corollary 35.2   Boys are able to predict the type of games their peers will choose with greater accuracy than girls. Social behavior which is manipulative of others is related in boys to the type of game in which they are engaged. In girls, this relationship does not hold true (28).

Corollary 35.3   Boyhood friendships are more likely to be based upon similarities in physical activity than are the friendships of girls (2, 7).

Corollary 35.4   By the age of 15, the social status of girls is largely independent of their ability to perform well in sports; the social acceptability of boys is largely dependent upon their skill in athletics (8).

Implications.   The emphasis that boys place upon athletic skill, and the manner in which it permeates their total value system, cannot be overlooked by coaches and classroom teachers. Whether the teacher considers this emphasis wrong or right is subordinate to the fact that *it exists.* This marked value judgment on the part of growing boys might at times be channeled into activities which will enhance their ability to *cognitively* manipulate their environment. Some have suggested that placing vigorous males and relatively passive females in the same classroom for learning experiences during childhood might be faulty pedagogy. It is a common observation of elementary school teachers that the active boy generally falls behind the cooperative girl. This suggests that a different approach might be taken to educating the boy during childhood than is taken when introducing the more passive girls to intellectual endeavors.

It is apparent that the use of games in aiding a child to become more socially acceptable to himself and to others is more effectively utilized with boys than girls. Teams which are formed tend to elicit friendships quickly among boys, and these friendships are in turn terminated and others made when new teams are formed.

The value system of girls, formed in part by cultural pressures, is more closely linked with such factors as appearance and verbal facility than with the ability to move. It was the author's recent experience, when he asked a group of girls in late childhood to "draw a picture of a little girl about your age," to receive only drawings of dismembered but attractive *heads* of girls. Boys in late childhood and early adolescence, on the other hand, will frequently submit drawings of idealized, muscular male figures.

36.0 Game participation by boys and girls forms a bridge between restrictive child rearing pressures and the assumption of adult roles in later life (28).

Play is therapeutic for children; it prepares them for various skills and roles in adult life, and at the same time serves as a buffer for various pressures imposed upon them by their parents. Restricted experiences in play may lead to mild or severe retardation in intellectual, emotional, and social development.

Corollary 36.1 Game choice and success in various types of games are related.

Success is pleasurable and leads to increased activity. People like to do the things they perceive themselves doing well. Increased motivation in motor activities accompanies increased competence, thus every effort should be made to enhance abilities as quickly as possible.

Corollary 36.2 Game choice in children may be a reflection of manner in which they are reared (28).

Certain theoreticians suggest that the manner in which children are reared is later reflected in the manner in which they play games and the type of games in which they select to engage. Children who have led highly restricted lives, with excessive parental control, may tend to seek relatively unstructured games involving an element of chance. On the other hand, families emphasizing success in the child rearing practices may tend to produce children who seek competitive games of skill in which chance has a smaller role in the final score achieved.

Corollary 36.3 Children are able to characterize their peers according to the type of game they habitually select and by the kind of behavior they usually choose to try to manipulate others (28).

Implications. The type of games children select to engage in are more than fun-seeking activities; they are a serious method of preparing themselves for adult life, and of relieving to some degree the pressures encountered from school and parents. A game *is* life to a child of five through ten. Success or failure in meeting peer expectations is thus as vital in the shaping of the child's personality (particularly a boy) as are the more important successes or failures encountered later in adolescence. Failure to perform well is crushing to a child's ego, while success at play has positive effects upon the child's concept of himself as a person valued by others.

Children observe each other closely in games, and behavior in games is one of the most direct ways in which they can evaluate each other's behavioral patterns. It is not surprising that game behavior, success in sports, and children's evaluations of each others' personal attributes are so closely related.

37.0   Cooperative and competitive behavior is trainable in children. Rewards for various kinds of competitive and cooperative behavior tend to mold the characteristic manner in in which a child approaches group situations (20).

Corollary 37.1   Imparting knowledge about desirable modes of group interaction has been shown to positively shift children into cooperative modes of behavior (17).

Implications. It is often voiced by physical educators and coaches that their goal is to teach "team work," and, in general, research indicates that this can be accomplished. The child is frequently faced with handling both competition and cooperation at the same time, as he is cooperating with his teammates while competing against another group. It has been found that sensitivity to problems relative to cooperative behavior is trainable. The result of this training has been shown to make children more productive in cooperative situations.

It is thus suggested that if the coach and physical educator desire, as an outcome of their programs, increased ability of the child to engage in cooperative behavior, the principles underlying productive group interaction must be outlined and not left to chance. Such training might include principles relating to group communication, group problem solving techniques, and the manner in which discussion should be led to encourage participation by all.

To expect children to automatically compete or cooperate effectively is not as realistic as expecting them to interact in these ways with the proper guidance. This guidance should not only take the form of instruction in inter-group relations at the level of understanding compatible with their maturational level, but also in the specific competitive and cooperative behaviors appropriate to the game at hand.

38.0 *The goals which indicate successful performance levels have been reached are influenced to a large degree by peer group behaviors. Goal-setting is modified by one's associates (3).*

Research studies have indicated that the manner in which children reward themselves for performances at various levels can be experimentally manipulated. Although there is some controversy concerning the extent to which peers, as opposed to parents, influence the value judgments and behavior of children and adolescents, the available evidence indicates that in physical skills, children influence one another in rather exact ways. Children and adolescents constantly set and revise performance standards which are acceptable to the group.

Sensitivity to the peer group's reward pattern should enable a coach and physical education teacher to make judicious choices of activities to include in physical education and athletic programs. Although the adult can be expected to exert some influence upon values and rewards connected with various types of physical performance, these adult values may only be introduced gradually into a given program. For example, if the physical educator feels that some kind of social or folk dance "belongs" in the physical education program, and the peer values with which he is surrounded are *not* compatible with such activities, he must proceed with caution and "sell" this component of his program to those in his charge.

39.0 *Reasonably predictable patterns denoting the acquisition of status and of leadership opportunities are detectable during childhood and adolescence (24).*

Corollary 39.1   Children with below average intelligence are not as concerned with the social implications of their performance as are children with average and above average intelligence (1).

Corollary 39.2   Social approval is linked more closely with gross motor skills than with fine motor skills in the case of male adolescents (9).

Corollary 39.3   As children begin to form groups for play, at about the age of five or six, physical prowess begins to enhance leadership potential (14, 24).

Corollary 39.4   The leadership of groups in childhood is obtained both through "bullying" (i.e., seizing power) and through more subtle manipulations (24).

Corollary 39.5   Extraversion is higher in boys whose physical skills are superior. Athletes score higher in measures of "confidence" (21).

Corollary 39.6   Children and early adolescent boys who acquire leadership roles influence their subordinates' acquisition of gestures, and at the same time the leaders assume movement characteristics which denote superiority (26).

Corollary 39.7   The assumption of leadership in street groups of male adolescents is partly dependent upon physical prowess.

Implications. To a large degree, the status hierarchy of children is dependent upon what a child can *do*—how well he can act in a rather obvious way. If leadership is bestowed upon that member of the group perceived as most capable of solving the group's problems, it is reasonable to expect that the problem which most concerns a group of growing children (males from 7 to 18) is one involving physical output. It is not surprising that those selected for leadership may be expected to possess, to some degree, the capability of dealing with the environment.

The obvious sex differences occurring in adolescence, relative to the value placed upon physical performance, of course, influence the acquisition of status. Female adolescents may sometimes acquire status through their association with the male athletic program by assuming the role of cheerleader.

A recent investigation dealing with late adolescents indicates how relatively ineffectual is the attempt to "make leaders" by exposing them to competition in physical endeavors (30). By the time a boy reaches late childhood and early adolescence, he is aware, within exact limits, of the nature of his physical abilities as related to those of his peers, and the extent to which these abilities will gain him status with his associates. Motivating the average or below average boy to perform by placing him into competitive situations during these adolescent years is not effective; he already knows how well he will finish in such competitions! Appealing to his desire for self-improvement, i.e., having him compete with himself and attempt to better his own previous performance, is probably a more constructive approach.

    40.0   *Normally a child of about four to five will begin to reflect the performance and movement characteristics of the like parent (12, 13).*

Corollary 40.1   Acceptability by a child's peers is not forthcoming if he has tended to identify with a member of the opposite sex and evidences inappropriate movement characteristics (12).

Corollary 40.2   Inappropriate movement characteristics will often be related to the presence of siblings of the opposite sex, and in boys will be manifested in poor performance in physical skills (12, 22).

Implications. Physical education teachers should be sensitive to the presence of boys and girls who need special assistance in the acquisition of movement patterns appropriate to members of their sex. Although at times the reasons for improper gender identification transcend the simple acquisition of gestures, walking, and throwing behavior, the physical educator can often aid the child in modifying the primary reason he is receiving social punishment from his peers by helping him adopt sex-appropriate performance characteristics. Training boys in proper throwing, running, and striking skills is helpful, while education in dance might aid girls who seem to have identified with their fathers to achieve more appropriate movement patterns. The male and female physical education teachers should be aware of the importance of themselves as "transmitting models" of behavior.

Summary

The child's needs for and training in social interactions are manifested in the games he plays and how he plays them. If no children are available, this need is manifested in the adoption of imaginary friends. If other children are present, the child finds joy in expressing himself through games and other less structured actions.

Children and adolescents utilize the actions of their peers as the main method of judging social acceptability. At least average physical skills are needed before a child can achieve status in his group. As adolescence is reached, even more emphasis is placed on physical achievements by boys in our culture.

Childhood games seem to provide an immature "slice" of the culture with which the child can experiment. In games, the child begins to experience his first feelings of social status or rejection, competition and cooperation, and success or failure. Adults on the fringes of the games should strive to make these initial experiences with life's interactions as productive as possible.

BIBLIOGRAPHY

1. Allport, Gordon, Murphy, Gardner, and May, Mary. *Memorandum on research in competition and cooperation.* New York: Social Science Research Council, 1937.

2. Austin, Mary C., and Thompson, George G. Children's friendships; a study of the basis on which children select and reject their best friends. *J. Ed. Psychol.,* 1948, 39, 101–116.

3. Bandura, Albert, and Kupers, Carol J. Transmission of patterns of self-reinforcement through modeling. *J. Abn. Soc. Psychol.,* 1964, 69, 1–9.

4. Bridges, D. M. B. *The social and emotional development of the pre-school child*. London: Routledge & Kegan Paul, 1931.

5. Britt, S. H., and James, S. Q. Toward a social psychology of human play. *J. Soc. Psychol.*, 1963, 23, 385–391.

6. Buhler, Charlotte. *Memorandum on research in competition and cooperation*. New York: Social Science Research Council, 1937.

7. Challman, Robert. Factors influencing friendships among pre-school children. *Child Dev.*, 1932, 3, 146–158.

8. Coleman, James S. *The adolescent Society*. New York: The Free Press of Glencoe, 1961.

9. Cratty, Bryant J., and Eachus, T. Correlates of personality and motor performance in two maze tasks. Paper presented to the National College Physical Education Association, 1961.

10. Gessell, A., *et al. Gessell developmental schedules*. New York: Psychological Corporation, 1949.

11. Goodenough, F. L., and Leahy, A. M. The effect of certain family relationships upon the development of personality. *J. Genet. Psychol.*, 1927, 34, 45–71.

12. Green, Richard, and Money, J. Effeminancy in prepubertal boys. *Pediatrics*, 1961, 27, 286–291.

13. Green, Richard, and Money, J. Tomboys and sissies. *Sexology*, 1961, 28, 113–115.

14. Greenberg, Pearl T. Competition in children; an experimental study. *Amer. J. Psychol.*, 1932, 44, 221–248.

15. Hardy, Martha C. Social recognition at the elementary school age. *J. Soc. Psychol.*, 1937, 8, 365–386.

16. Hartrup, W. W. Friendship status and the effectiveness of peers as reinforcing agents. *J. of Exp. Child Psychol.*, 1962, 1, 154–162.

17. Heise, Bryan. Effects of instruction in cooperation on the attitudes and conduct of children. Ann Arbor: University of Michigan Press, 1942.

18. Horwitz, Murray. The recall of interrupted group tasks; an experimental study of individual motivation in relation to group goals. *Human Relations*, 1953, 6, 145–162.

19. Hunt, J. M., and Solomon, R. L. The stability and some correlates of group status in a summer camp group of young boys. *Amer. J. Psychol.*, 1942, 55, 33–45.

20. Jack, L. M. An experimental study of ascendant behavior in pre-school children. *University of Iowa Studies of Child Welfare*, 1934, 3, 50–65.

21. Kagan, Jerome, and Moss, H. A. *Birth to maturity; a study in psychological development*. New York: Wiley, 1962.

22. Koch, H. L. Sissiness and tomboyishness in relation to sibling characteristics. *J. Genet. Psychol.*, 1956, 88, 231–284.

23. Missiurio, W. The development of reflex activity in children, in *International research in sport and physical education*, E. Jokl (ed.). Springfield, Illinois: Chas. C. Thomas, 1964, 372–383.

24. Parten, Mildred B. Leadership among pre-school children. *J. Abn. and Soc. Psychol.*, 1933, 28, 136–147.

25. Parten, Mildred B. Social play among pre-school children. *J. Abn. and Soc. Psychol.*, 1933, 27, 430–440.

26. Pitney, R. Rorlando, and Freeman, H. Personality and attitudinal similarity among classmates. *J. Appl. Psychol.*, 1932, 21, 48–65.

27. Ryan, E. Dean. Competitive performance in relation to achievement motivation and anxiety. Paper presented to the National Association of Health, Physical Education, and Recreation, Minneapolis, Minnesota, 1963.

28. Sutton-Smith, B., and Robert, J. M. Rubrics of competitive behavior. *J. Genet. Psychol.*, 1964, 34, 119–126.

29. Tuddenham, R. D. Studies in reputation III: correlates of popularity among elementary school children. *J. Educ. Psychol.*, 1951, 42, 257–276.

30. Werner, Alfred C., and Gottheil, Edward. Personality development, and participation in college athletics. *Res. Quart.*, 1966, 37, 126–131.

The family exerts an early and profound influence upon the child; it assigns him a role, punishes and rewards him for various kinds of behavior, and molds his values. While it might appear farfetched to examine some of the principles governing the influence of the family upon the child in a text concerned with psychological principles in physical education, it is believed important for the physical educator to be aware of the various ways in which the family can influence the child in situations calling for vigorous physical output.

Interactions within the family are complex, and include relationships between the child and each parent, the parents' feelings about the child, and interactions with his siblings. The ordinal placement of the child in the family as well as the sex and age of brothers and sisters are all important. Values transmitted by close relatives often directly influence the manner in which the child behaves in situations of interest to the coach and physical educator. The educator will often say that it is *he* who is the molder of the children and youth placed in his charge. However, a powerful group of people enter the child's life prior to his exposure to the educator. It is the purpose, in the pages which follow, to examine some findings which relate to the influence these people have upon the movement behavior of their offspring.

6 The Family and the Child

41.0   *More influential of the child's personality than child rearing practices are the feelings parents have toward their offspring.*

Corollary 41.1   Parental acceptance of and love toward their children are related directly to their feelings about each other (13).

Corollary 41.2   Parental hostility and overcontrol elicit hostility on the part of the child (8, 10, 13).

Corollary 41.3   The amount of control exerted and the amount of love parents have toward a child are not necessarily related. Less parental control is exerted as the child matures; however, the amount of parental love extended remains relatively consistent over the years (13).

Corollary 41.4   Parents are more likely to tolerate aggression on the part of their children toward siblings and peers than aggression directed toward themselves (13, 14).

Implications.   Some experts have suggested that the extent to which the child has had an opportunity to express aggressions and the experiences a child has had when expressing aggressions relate directly to the manner in which he releases his hostilities in sports when a young adult. For example, some foreign authorities in sports psychology have suggested that early experience connected with the expression of aggressions which have been unpleasant is later reflected in a disinclination to compete vigorously in athletics. Such people find it difficult to fully extend themselves in sports; they seem afraid of channeling their aggressions in an all-out manner when competing. Specifically, it is stated, this seems manifested in athletes who, upon reaching a point of imminent victory, withdraw and accept defeat.

Although such a hypothesis is open to question, it is apparent that athletics provide a relatively innocuous, socially approved vehicle in which the child and youth may express aggressions which would be punished if directed toward parents or peers in other forms. The "drainage theory," which suggests that physical activity represents a healthy outlet for aggressions, is finding less favor with child development experts. They have recently declared that training in such sports as judo and boxing often merely incite the child to higher levels of excitation, which may be harmful to his personality. Thus, while physical activities may not "drain" aggressions, they at least provide a relatively harmless and at times statusful manner of redirecting them. Many of these aggressions could have arisen from overcontrol, rejection, and/or hostility on the part of the child's parents.

42.0   *Various amounts of physical control are exercised over the actions of children in primitive cultures and in modern cultures.*

There is little evidence, however, that even rather severe physical restriction, e.g., placing Indian children in cradles for extended periods of time, either limits or elicits unusual amounts of physical activity later in life (4, 14).

Corollary 42.1   Studies have demonstrated that marked differences exist among the amounts of physical control various mothers exert over their offspring relative to the amount of playing area around the home permitted, the vigor of indoor physical activity allowed, and the amount of monitoring over the child's playing time (14).

Some mothers restrict the child's movements to within a short distance of the home, while others permit more freedom of movement. Some parents check frequently concerning their child's whereabouts; on the other hand, others exert no such control. It has also been found that, within the home, differences in parental controls are apparent concerning the amount of physical activity permitted. Some parents do not permit any vigorous activity in the home, others specify that only certain places in the home shall be used as indoor gymnasia, whereas others permit rather free movements within the home. It is difficult to believe that these differences in the amount of physical control do not directly influence the child's attitudes toward physical activity, and, similarly, development of perceptual-motor attributes on the part of the children involved.

Corollary 42.2   It has been hypothesized that the early motoric development which has been measured in Negro babies in Africa, as compared to the development evidenced by Caucasian babies in the United States, is attributable to the early and prolonged physical contact between mother and child during the early child rearing months within the former group (9, 19).

Implications. The literature relating early child rearing practices to physical restriction fails to demonstrate that later physical development in children is related to physical restriction (even to the point of keeping a baby bound for the first months of life by certain American Indians of the 1930's).

The early tactile communication the child receives from his mother seems to have a positive effect upon his motor development. The bulk of the literature indicates that early maternal attention to the child in the form of caressing has a desirable influence upon general psychological development, evidenced into late adolescence. Deprivation of these early contacts, on the other hand, seems to have a negative effect upon the perceptual motor development of the child.

It has been suggested that members of certain racial groups engage more in helpful parent-child play with their young offspring than do others. Furthermore, it has also been asserted that this kind of activity can produce children who are better equipped with physical skills.

Corollary 42.3   Early maternal deprivation prior to the age of six months has been demonstrated to produce lethargic behavior, some perceptual disturbances, and generally apathetic social behavior later in adolescence (5).

Implications. It would seem that the physical educator-coach makes a rather belated contact with the youth, at a time in the child's life after many important forces have already begun to mold his energy level and general proclivity toward physical activity. It is apparent that for physical educators to make a real contribution to the physical development of infants and children, they should attempt to devise programs of motor activities in which parents and infants can begin engaging during the first few months of life. There is apparently a wide difference in the amount of movement encouraged in infants by their parents during these early months. Specific programs of activities to enhance an infant's perceptual-motor attributes should prove helpful to the parent who will not "naturally" engage in frequent play with children.

> **43.0**   *In children as young as three, parents have begun to lose some of their ability to reward performance by extending their approval (15).*

Corollary 43.1   A female experimenter is more influential of a female child's performance than is the presence of a parent (15).
Corollary 43.2   Strangers have been demonstrated to elicit better performance than parents in an experimental situation (15).

Implications. With constant exposure to a rewarding or punishing stimulus (i.e., the parent), the stimulus loses some of its negative or positive reinforcing qualities. The constant pressure and presence of a parent is often "blocked out" by children, and better performance in specific situations can often be elicited by teachers and others with whom the child comes in contact. From the foregoing, the importance of the teacher-coach's role is obvious.

The influence of a mature male model is particularly great upon goal-setting and performance of boys from the ages of eight to fifteen. While parents exert an early and basic influence upon the child, the physical educator-coach has an important role in molding the child's interests and performance levels in obvious ways. The child will change under the influences of a mature male coach. The direction of that change should be the critical concern of everyone connected with physical activity.

44.0 To varying degrees, parents engage in self-reliance train-ing of their children. Parents instill in their children, in rather specific ways, a conception of which tasks are worthwhile pursuing (12).

Self-reliance training takes the form of goal-setting and of giving general directions when the child is engaged in problem-solving behavior. Parents doing this well seem to be pulling the child from ahead rather than pushing from behind. If this goal-setting is reasonable, and if direc-tions which encourage thought in the child are extended, high aspiring children are produced.

Corollary 44.1 Aspiration levels of parents are related to the aspiration levels of their children (12).

Corollary 44.2 Children who have been subjected to self-reliance training require less assistance when attempting new tasks; they refuse directions which are too detailed and prefer the challenge of the unknown. They generally achieve more than children who are not trained in this way (12).

Corollary 44.3 Children who have had self-reliance training perform at higher levels than children who have not been encouraged in this way (12).

Implications. Investigation has indicated that this type of training influences the performance of both mental and motor tasks. High needs for achievement are characteristic of children whose parents have con-tinually set goals which "stretch," but do not frustrate, their offspring. Critical in raising boys' needs for achievement are the comments and behavior of their fathers (12).

A vital type of motive which influences the behavior of humans is re-lated to their needs for achievement rather than to physiological needs. In modern society, basic nutritional needs are usually met. Achievement and performance are more dependent upon the individual's feelings about mastering a task for the sake of achievement alone. Further discussion con-cerning achievement need is found in Part Three. In summary, however, it is clear that parents engage in behavior which molds their children's desires to aspire high, to attempt to achieve consistently in a variety of ways. The child whom the coach-physical educator cannot seem to moti-vate may be a victim of inappropriate parental training rather than being apathetic because of some shortcoming of the educator or the situation.

45.0 Moderately high father-son correlations are seen when com-paring their locomotor abilities, e.g., running and broad-

jumping. On the other hand, activities which involve primarily the arms and eyes (e.g., throwing and vaulting) evidence little similarity between father and son (3).

Implications. Although the research is far from conclusive on this point, it would appear that the high school track coach would be correct to make a broad survey relative to basic ability to run and to jump when selecting boys for the team. On the other hand, coaches of other sports (basketball, tennis, and others in which skilled learning is essential) would seem best advised to recruit individuals who are highly motivated to spend time learning the intricacies of the activity.

It is difficult to separate father-son influences due to inheritance from those influences which are primarily social. Does the son tend to run fast and jump high and far because he has been exposed to the activities by a father who achieved success in them? Or are they inherent qualities that the father has passed on to his son? It is probable that both inherent and environmental factors are operative to some degree.

46.0   *Nursery school age boys who are relatively passive in play activities and are reinforced in intellectual endeavors by their mothers tend to evidence less aggressive kinds of behavior in adolescence and early adulthood (8).*

Longitudinal studies of children from birth to the age of 25 indicate that the passive male can be differentiated from the active one rather early in life. The extent to which vigorous activity is engaged in during the nursery school years is indicative of the kind of personality traits which will emerge in late adolescence and early adulthood. Similarly, occupational choice can be predicted, categorically, by noting the nature of a child's behavior in the nursery school play yard.

After boys enter school they are not easily classifiable into active versus passive categories; school seems to have a suppressing effect upon their natural level of activity. On the other hand, their pre-school behavior seems moderately related to levels of activation in early adulthood.

47.0   *Play equipment provided by the family does not seem to have a measurable influence upon the fitness or level of activity exhibited by the children (14).*

The effective use of play equipment has been attributed to the presence of older siblings; at the same time, the presence of play equipment has been demonstrated to elicit more social interaction between children. The mere presence of equipment in the home, however, is not enough. Some-one must be present as an instructor or stimulating friend or parent in order for the equipment to exert a significant influence over the capacities and activity levels of children using it. Indeed, in poorer social-economic groups in which there is a notable absence of backyard play equipment, activity levels and fitness are noticeably greater. Children in this lower economic category react much as do primitive tribes; they provide their own equipment by modifying the materials at hand and evidence, in a creative way, the ability to "make do" with what inexpensive objects are available.

It would seem, therefore, that the mere presence of play equipment is not as important as the presence of others who help to form positive or negative attitudes about the use of the equipment. The manner in which status can be gained in its effective use is also influential of the importance of such equipment to the physical development of children.

48.0   *Inappropriate gender identification may be the result of early and faulty human imprinting (6).*

It is often suggested that the absence of an effective male model contributes to the inability of young boys to adopt appropriate masculine patterns of behavior and, specifically, to perform physical skills in a masculine way. Feminine boys usually incur a great deal of social punishment from their peers.

Physical educators often feel threatened by the presence of such boys in their classes and, like the peers, frequently subject them to ridicule or ignore them. Feminine boys' first confrontation with the necessity to perform well in games can be a traumatic experience for them. It is the obligation of physical educators not only to offer them emotional encouragement but also to provide them with specific assistance in the acquisition of sex appropriate skills which they need to insure peer acceptance.

It is not unreasonable to hypothesize that proficiency in motor skill can exert at least an indirect influence upon the assumption of behavior denoting proper gender identification. It has been frequently noted by the author, and verified in interviews with children and their parents, that boys who evidence behavioral patterns which are feminine report that they have simply withdrawn from the boys' games as their ineptitudes are commented upon, and have begun to play with the girls, from whom they receive support rather than punishment. It has been well documented that individuals interacting in close proximity pick up the gesture patterns of those with whom they are interacting. Thus it is probable that at least one of the causes for the assumption of behavior denoting improper gender identification in boys may stem from frequent association with girls for the reason stated above.

49.0   *Child rearing practices seem to influence the type of games children and adults habitually choose.*

Some researchers have recently hypothesized that the manner in which a child has been reared, the amount of control exerted as well as the values instilled, influences the nature of the games the child will seek. Although this assumption needs further research, several implications may be drawn from this theory.

Corollary 49.1   When child rearing for responsibility is emphasized, games emphasizing chance may be engaged in during later life (16, 17).

Corollary 49.2   When achievement is emphasized, especially in the case of boys, games involving strategy and skill may be more likely to be selected in childhood and adolescence (16).

Corollary 49.3   Members of higher socio-economic groups may be more likely to engage in games of strategy and skill. Members of lower socio-economic groups, since their achievements are seldom rewarded, may tend to select games of chance in which "lady luck" has the opportunity to be equally benevolent to all (16, 17).

It is generally believed that the best athletic teams will be found in underprivileged communities in which athletics provide one of the few opportunities for financial and social success. There may be a point, however, at which poverty tends to limit ambition, even in athletes. On the other hand, individuals from the middle levels of society, having been subjected from their early years to the axiom that "hard work brings success," are likely to engage vigorously in games and sports which emphasize skill and strategy.

Members of extremely disadvantaged groups, it has been hypothesized, will tend to engage in games of chance with some frequency. Through this means they put their trust in luck, rather than depending upon their own skill and fortitude, which may seem to them unlikely to bring any upward social mobility.

Summary

Although the literature relating specific child rearing practices to physical capacity and performance measures of children is extremely sparse, there are indications that early parental influences of an emotional nature motivate general aspiration levels and achievement needs that children evidence. The physical educator is, to some degree, confined by the kinds of early experiences to which the children and youth on his teams and in his classes have been subjected.

Children may at times tend to reject the constantly punishing or rewarding parent, and affix their allegiance on another mature figure who more objectively rewards or punishes their successes and failures—the teacher-coach. Sensitivity on the part of the educator to the marked influence he may have upon the values of children and adolescents should lead to greater responsibility when selecting the kinds of things he points his charges towards and the methods he chooses for them when competing in athletic endeavors.

The literature on child rearing must sometimes be discounted. Much of the research, for example, hinges upon the often unreliable parental report. Parents tend to report to child development experts the kinds of things they feel are desirable. More than one investigator has, upon requestioning parents regarding their child rearing practices, found that different answers were forthcoming several years later.

It would seem beneficial if the physical educator and coach, when attempting to elicit superior performance from a boy or a girl in his charge, would take a closer look at the manner in which the child and his parents interact. If the parents seem to be exerting an influence negative to that desired, parental conferences between the coach and the parent may be as desirable as the meetings usually recommended between classroom teachers and parents.

BIBLIOGRAPHY

1. Anderson, Harold H. Domination and integration in the social behavior of young children. *Genet. Psychol. Monog.*, 1937, 19, 343–408.
2. Anderson, Harold H., and Brandt, H. F. Study of motivation involving self-announced goals of fifth grade children of the concept of level of aspiration. *J. Soc. Psychol.*, 1939, 10, 209–232.
3. Cratty, B. J. A comparison of fathers and sons in physical ability. *Res. Quart.*, 1960, 31, 12–15.
4. Dennis, Wayne. Infant development under conditions of restricted practice and of minimum social stimulation. *Genet. Psychol. Monog.*, 1941, 23, 143–189.
5. Goldfarb, W. Effects of psychological deprivation in infancy and subsequent stimulation. *Amer. J. Psychiat.*, 1945, 102, 18–22.
6. Green, Richard, and Money, J. Tomboys and sissies. *Sexology*, 1961, 28, 113–115.
7. Jones, H. E. Order of birth in relation to the development of the child, in *A handbook of child psychology*, C. Murchison (ed.). Worcester: Clark University Press, 1931, 204–241.

8. Kagan, Jerome, and Moss, H. A. *Birth to maturity: a psychological study.* New York: Wiley, 1962.

9. Knoblock, Hilda, and Pasamanick, Benjamin. Further observations on the behavioral development of Negro children. *J. Genet. Psychol.*, 1953, 83, 137–157.

10. Orlansky, H. Infant care and personality. *Psychol. Bull.*, 1949, 46, 1–48.

11. Roberts, J. M., Arth, J., and Bush, R. R. Games in culture. *Amer. Anthropol.*, 1959, 61, 597–605.

12. Rosen, Bernard C., and D'Andrade, Roy. The psychosocial origins of achievement motivation. *Sociometry*, 1959, 22, 185–218.

13. Schaefer, E. S., and Bell, R. Q. Patterns of attitudes toward child rearing and the family. *J. Abn. Soc. Psychol.*, 1957, 54, 391–395.

14. Sears, Robert R., MacCoby, Eleanor E., and Levin, Harry. *Patterns of child rearing.* Evanston: Row, Peterson, and Co., 1957.

15. Stevenson, H. W., Kleen, R., and Knights, Robert M. Parents and strangers as reinforcing agents for children's performance. *J. Abn. Soc. Psychol.*, 1963, 67, 183–186.

16. Sutton-Smith, B., Roberts, J. M., and Kozelka, Robert M. Game involvement in adults. *J. of Soc. Psychol.*, 1963, 60, 15–30.

17. Sutton-Smith, B., and Rosenberg, B. G. *Play and game list.* Bowling Green, Ohio: Bowling Green State University Press, 1959.

18. Toman, Walter. *Family constellation.* New York: Springer Publishing Co., 1961.

19. Williams, Judith R., and Scott, Roland B. Growth and development of Negro infant IV: motor development and its relationship to child rearing practices in two groups of Negro infants. *Child Dev.* 1953, 24, 103–121.

part three

MOTIVATION

About one-third of the literature in experimental psychology during the past 50 years has been concerned with various problems connected with motivation. Many of these investigations have utilized humans as subjects, while some have attempted to draw conclusions relative to human motivation by assessing the behavior of food-deprived rats.

Early experimenters suggested that all attempts to explain why individuals select and persist in various undertakings must depend upon drives related to satisfaction of basic physiological needs involving the seeking of food, sex, and so on. More recent writers, however, have developed theoretical frameworks which incorporate an expanded list of reasons to explain the direction and persistence of human activity. These latter theories frequently allude to needs for achievement, social recognition, status, and similar concepts.

Motivation can be considered in several dimensions. Motives can be defined as factors or conditions which influence events or objects that are *selected* for attention. Motives attempt to explain the *intensity* with which individuals engage in something and/or the effort *sustained* in some activity.

At the same time, motivation can be considered on a time dimension relative to performance of some kind of task. Initially, motivation relates to the general state of arousal and subsequent level of attention paid to a problem or task facing an individual. This initial reaction or orientation has often been referred to as *activa-*

7 The Nature of Human Motivation

tion, implying that certain muscular-physiologic changes occur as the human selects and regards some component of his environment with which he may interact (5).

Motives can be described as factors which impinge upon the human *while* he performs. They tend to influence the intensity with which he engages in an activity, and are also considered factors which determine how long he will persist in difficult tasks.

Finally, motivation can be said to relate to the self-evaluation a person makes relative to success or failure in meeting some goal. These evaluations usually influence how soon he will attempt to perform the task again, or whether he will ever again attack the task and, if so, with what intensity (1).

These definitions of motivation involve an interrelation between psychological and physiological factors. Pre-task muscular tension, for example, is accompanied by changes in respiration and blood chemistry which prepare the body for action.

Other terms and concepts are closely related to motivation. *Tension,* for example, is an important indication of a general heightening of the organism's level of activation. *Arousal level* is usually dependent upon the point on several physiological-biological cycles at which the individual is momentarily functioning. These fluctuations are as short as a heart beat or as long as several months. Some, such as the 24 hour sleep period or the menstrual cycle, are easily identifiable, while others are not as clearly delineated. In any case, the individual's general state of alertness and motivation to perform is to some degree influenced by the point on these cycles during which performance takes place. For example, studies in the 1930's which attempted to ascertain the time of day most conducive to superior performance concluded that tasks carried out during the morning hours (at about 10 A.M.) would produce scores superior to the same motor tasks engaged in during the late afternoon.

Anxiety and stress are also related to motivation. Fear of failure in a task has an important influence upon the individual's feelings about subsequent efforts in the same or similar undertakings. In general, motivation is negatively affected if performance and conditions related to performance are stressful to the individual. Social stress is merely another way of describing the negative motivation in a performance situation witnessed by those capable of appraising or disapproving the individual's efforts.

In the following pages, the statements will relate to some general concepts underlying the study of motivation, and the effect of various kinds of variables upon selection of activities, intensity with which they are performed, and length of time during which performance in various motor activities may persist. Chapter 8 contains statements which more specifically pinpoint the influence of several kinds of motives upon perceptual-motor functioning.

50.0   One of the primary motivating factors of children, youth, and adults performing perceptual-motor skills is the desire for mastery of a task to satisfy a basic achievement need (1).

Although initially it might be hypothesized that an individual learns to perform well on the job to satisfy needs for a home, sexual fulfillment, and other basic physiological drives, with increased exposure to the job, motivation to do well at the task itself will tend to become functionally independent of the original reasons for engaging in it.

Corollary 50.1   In an affluent modern society, individuals seldom perform sports skills to satisfy basic physiological needs (1).

It is constantly apparent when observing humans in experimental situations that they improve simply because a challenge has been transmitted. Subjects volunteer for research studies, and will evidence performance improvement whether or not pay or some other reward (e.g., class credit) is present in the situation.

Although this phenomenon has been explained in various ways, humans seem simply to react to situations which tax their perceptual-motor abilities, and attempt to solve complex problems and learn complex skills simply because they find satisfaction in exercising their capacities. Improvement will usually occur independent of any obvious rewards or degrees of social approval. Humans seem to find pleasure in imbalancing their physiological mechanism, and at times seem to seek moderate amounts of stress in the form of vigorous and complex physical activities.

Implications.   Inherent in the offerings of physical educators and coaches are certain built-in motives. Physical educators can elicit maximum effort by selecting activities for presentation to children and youth which are challenging and stretch their abilities, rather than by employing those which are relatively simple and uncomplicated.

Such a principle also suggests that many individuals may find satisfaction simply in self-improvement rather than in beating others. This is particularly noted when working with mature university-age youth and attempting to motivate them to improve their skills. The writer, several years ago, found that college swimming classes, when polled concerning the kinds of things that occurred in the class which allegedly helped them learn, declared that they were motivated, not by competing with each other, but by striving for self-improvement.

Social stress can be applied at times to elicit performance increments in the immature. However, more mature performers will react more favorably, it is believed, when an appeal is made to their pride in personal achievement. The implications of these statements for the athletic coach at the high school and the college-university level are clear.

Football coaches, for example, frequently devise individual scoring systems denoting how well defensive as well as offensive players carry out their assignments on each play. Using such a device, a player may chart his improvement from game to game, independent of team victories or defeats.

Similarly, boys and girls in physical education classes at the secondary and university levels are probably more interested in individual improvement than their ranking with the group. By adolescence, individuals know within exact limits their abilities on a variety of motor tasks; self-improvement is a more motivating way to approach individuals in these class situations. Individual scoring systems based upon the activities participated in would also be helpful in this latter context.

> **51.0**   *There is an optimum level of motivation desirable for best performance in a given task (5).*

Corollary 51.1   Individuals scoring within the middle ranges on a scale purporting to evaluate anxiety tend to perform best in complex coordination tasks (6).
Corollary 51.2   Optimum degrees of muscular tension (usually 50-75 per cent maximum) elicited by performing some kind of muscular task, e.g., squeezing a hand dynamometer, improve ability to memorize lists of letters and words (3).
Corollary 51.3   There is an optimum amount of tension generated prior to the task which will result in optimum performance (5).

Implications. It is believed that the above statements are among the most important in the text. The coach and instructor who is sensitive to individual levels of tension prior to and during performance of a task, seeks ways of removing or impeding tension, and, at the same time, raises the tension levels of individuals who appear to possess too little, will elicit better performance from his subordinates.

The ability to raise and lower motivational levels of performers via verbal exhortation or verbal pacification is one of the most desired qualities in a coach or physical educator. The individual performer himself is often seen attempting to "get himself up" for the task confronting him prior to its performance. The extent to which the performer can accomplish adjustment of pre-task tension within himself also contributes to personal success in athletic skills.

Critical to raising or lowering tension levels of participants are: (*a*) knowledge of how much tension is optimum for a given task, (*b*) aware-

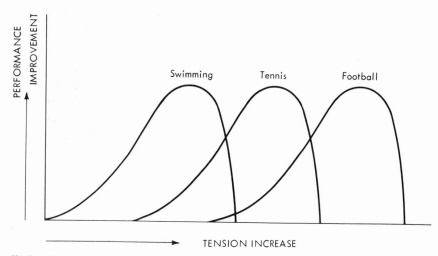

Fig. 3. *Optimum Tension for Various Sports. There is more tension generally necessary for actions in which an interior lineman in American football engages, slightly less for the movements of a tennis player, and much less for recreational swimming.*

ness of the amount of tension present within a given performer's psychological makeup, (c) sensitivity to the kinds of things which can be counted upon to raise or lower an individual's level of motivation relative to the task at hand. Some of the statements which follow in this chapter relate to these considerations.

There are innumerable ways in which a physical educator or coach can adjust the tension level of participants in his charge. Arranging for inter-team competitions between members of nearly equal ability is one frequently used technique. A comparison of players via the individual scoring systems mentioned previously is another. Verbal admonishment will serve to raise tension levels if they are less than optimum; however, this technique should usually be applied to individuals rather than to groups whose individual members may react differently to the same verbal punishment.

52.0   *Motives for performance are often transitory; conditions which can be counted upon to inspire superior performance at one time may not work at a later date (1).*

People seem constantly surrounded by a "constellation" of values, any one of which may impinge upon individual needs to perform well at a given time. At times, athletes subjected to the apparently motivating stress of competition (or similar variables) over a period of time lose their enthusiasm, and tend to block out reasons which in the past helped them to do well.

Implications. Coaches and teachers should be constantly aware of the possibility of personal shifts in motivations, and be sensitive to the possible directions of these shifts. Continual exhortation by the coach during half-time of early season football games, emphasizing one kind of motive, may begin to lose its effect toward the middle of the season. New avenues of approach must be utilized with children and youth as they perform for extended periods of time. Initial appeals to needs for peer status might give way to emphasis upon individual self-improvement during the latter part of a sports season.

The critical requirement for the coach is to ascertain just what it is that motivates a given athlete at a given time. Although the psychoanalyst might recommend extended therapy to uncover deep-seated complexes of motives, the coach has neither the time nor the background to accomplish this. In several experimental studies, the most reliable method of assessing motivation during the performance and learning of tasks resembling those found in athletic programs was to ask the students. It would seem that a few minutes spent with sports performers by the coach might yield good results if he simply asks them!

Humans are not simply animals to be exercised; they are constantly evaluating the social implications of their successes or failures in sports. Failure to examine at some length the kinds of reasons each individual on a team has for being there in the first place and the degree to which he seems to be trying would seem to result in considerably less than optimum performance on the part of the group and of individuals of the group.

> **53.0**   *Raising an individual's level of motivation results in measurable physiological changes, raises the tension level in muscle groups specific to the task, and heightens general bodily tension (5).*

Corollary 53.1   Raising an individual's tension level results in improved performance in simple, direct acts, while at times it impedes performance in complex acts which require more complex judgments (5).

Corollary 53.2   Raising an individual's tension level through some kind of verbal exhortation, introduction of competition, and similar means will improve performance in complex acts if the individual has been performing at a tension level which is below optimum, and will impede performance if he is already performing at optimum tension level for a given task (5).

Corollary 53.3   The tension requirements of tasks vary markedly; at the same time, desirable tension requirements of a given task change as it is learned (7).

Implications. Conditions introduced to motivate a performer during the initial stages of a task may not be appropriate during the final stages of the task. In general, tension levels tend to decrease as a complex act is learned, although at times tension will increase toward the end of the learning process if a known success criterion is to be achieved. The instructor should be sensitive to the fact that he may have to vary the direction of his efforts when attempting to elicit maximum performance from individuals as they reach higher performance levels through practice.

It is equally important for the instructor to consider the approximate amounts of tension appropriate for a given task as compared to other tasks, and also to compare appropriate tension needed for various positions and functions on a team. For example, it is seldom possible to engender too much tension in interior linemen performing a pass-protection block in American football. However, surplus tension can seriously disrupt the more exact perceptual-motor skill of the quarterback as he drops back to pass.

> **54.0** *Social motives invariably take precedence over tissue needs as individuals perform various sports skills* (1).

Corollary 54.1   The personality trait, "need for social approval," is frequently related to performance in various gross motor tasks (4).

Corollary 54.2   Social status may be gained or lost through successful performance in sports skills, particularly on the part of the males in our society (2).

Success in athletics is one of the more certain ways for male adolescents to win social approval. Status levels achieved for participation on athletic teams are seldom gained in any other way.

Implications. The coach-teachers have at their disposal one of the most powerful motives within the value system of the male adolescent. The youth can be "molded" by coaches in ways which other educators with whom he comes in contact cannot accomplish. The high school gymnasium provides a place wherein the male adolescent can prove his "manhood," gain acceptance and high status from his peers, and in other ways enhance his social image. Through this important avenue, the coach and teacher have an obligation to attempt to enhance achievement in more scholarly endeavors given status by the society during the adolescent's later years.

The coach-physical educator has an obligation, however, not only to exploit the social pressures in the situation when attempting to elicit winning performance, but also to emphasize *personal* pride in achievement. The youth performing in athletics is usually acutely aware of the extent to which the remainder of the school, the community, and his parents are viewing his performance; thus emphasis on social motives may be redundant. Youthful performers should be given a sense of pride in achievement and in the fact that success means all-out effort, regardless of community reaction to their win-loss records.

Moderate achievement in certain sports activities frequently enhances the social acceptance of adults. Moderate to good ability in golf, tennis, and swimming can relate to job success. Individuals seldom exercise because of a real cognitive awareness of the physiological benefits of exercise to the human organism. Rather, they participate in recreational sports because they may gain the approval of others, and in other ways enhance their social acceptability.

> **55.0** Anxiety about performing, resulting in lowered motivation, is seldom related to the physical harm an individual may incur when engaged in the task; rather, such fears invariably relate to the social consequences of failure (2).

Implications. Participation in a given task under varying degrees of social pressure presents a situation with both negative and positive forces interacting at the same time. Many activities prove threatening, not because of the real physical harm which may transpire, e.g., being injured on the football team, but because of the social stigma attached to failing, e.g., failing to make the starting line-up.

It is far easier to avoid performance situations in which one may *lose* prestige than to seek them to gain prestige. Fear of failure (failure anxiety) is many times the most difficult kind of problem for the coach to meet. Individuals afflicted with it, if they appear on the athletic scene at all, stop trying if the situation becomes too threatening. They will often stop short of winning because winning poses the additional obligation of winning again.

Sensitivity to punishing as well as rewarding components of the sports situation which confront the prospective performer should help to eliminate some of the performance blocks caused by anxieties about social punishment connected with the perceived possibility of failure. The coach should attempt to point out to individuals and teams the primary source of their anxieties, if these fears seem to be piling up to the detriment of performance. At times the situation may call for the coach to demonstrate to the team how insignificant the impending game is within the context of the performer's total life experiences.

Summary

The preceding pages have attempted to illustrate some of the interrelationships between such concepts as activation, arousal, motivation, anxiety, stress, and social pressure. Although these ideas are usually divisible experimentally, in a sports situation they are often so closely related that they are inseparable to the observer. An individual's motives to perform are a function of his general anxiety about success or failure, the particular point upon which he is momentarily residing in an underlying cycle of arousal, and his reaction to the social pressures within the situation.

Muscular tension, obviously related to physical performance, is influenced by the general level of activation and the specific kinds of motives impinging upon the performer. The problem for the coach and physical educator attempting to elicit optimum performance is to ascertain the motivational level of the performer—the tension requirements of the task —and, at the same time, ascertain to what personal motives he should appeal when preparing the performer for action.

It is usually easier to raise tension levels in sports performers than to lower them. The very presence of the crowd and the performer's perceptions of the social implications of failure or success are enough to send soaring the physiological mechanisms which support his activity level.

Specific programs to elicit relaxation in individuals and groups should be helpful adjuncts to some performance situations. These programs should be well planned, and may immediately precede games or be incorporated into daily workouts.

Some of the statements in Chapter 8 deal more specifically with various means through which the motivational state of the performer may be adjusted both upwards and downwards.

BIBLIOGRAPHY

1. Atkinson, J. W. Toward experimental analysis of human motivation in terms of motives, expectancies, and incentives, in *Motives in fantasy, action and society,* J. W. Atkinson (ed.). Princeton, N.J.: Van Nostrand, 1958.

2. Basowitz, H., Persky, H., Korchin, S. J., and Grinker, R. R. *Anxiety and stress: an interdisciplinary study of a life situation.* New York: McGraw-Hill, 1955.

3. Courts, F. A. Relations between muscular tension and performance. *Psychol. Bull.,* 1942, 39, 347–367.

4. Cratty, Bryant J., and Eachus, T. Correlates of personality and motor performance in two maze tasks. Paper presented at the College Physical Education Assn., Kansas City, 1961.

5. Duffy, Elizabeth. *Activation and behavior.* New York: Wiley, 1962.

6. Matarazzo, Ruth, and Matarazzo, J. D. Anxiety level and pursuit rotor performance. *J. Consult. Psychol.*, 1956, 20, 70.

7. Stroud, J. B. The role of muscular tension in stylus maze learning. *J. Exp. Psychol.*, 1931, 14, 606–631.

8. Woodworth, R. S. *Dynamics of behavior.* New York: Holt, 1958, 403.

It is proposed in this chapter to examine critically some of the motives that purport to enhance or detract from human performance. Some of these, under two sets of circumstances, will either raise *or* lower the individual's capacity and/or inclination to perform. Some of the motives relate to the social context in which the performance occurs, while others are inherent in the nature of the activity.

Although it has been attempted to describe practical situations in which the influence of motives may be evidenced, the reader is urged to utilize the following statements as bases for discussion, and to attempt to draw from his own experiences instances which either confirm or deny the truth of the statements presented. The study of motivation is extremely complex; scholars of human behavior are still awaiting a theoretical explanation for all of the factors which are observed to modify the performance of humans and animals.

Several individuals may be impelled to perform the same task in the same way and with the same intensity for different reasons. At the same time, if several people are given the same apparent motive to perform, a variety of behavior will be elicited. To talk about human motivation in absolute terms would be naive, but to ignore motivation when studying skilled motor performance is a serious oversight.

8 Analysis of Motives

56.0 *Competition may either enhance or detract from performance.*

Corollary 56.1   Competition raises the tension level of a performer, and thus can be expected to improve simple forceful acts and to detract from complex performance if the individual is already working at an appropriate tension level (13).

Corollary 56.2   The effect of competition upon performance is partly a function of the personality makeup of the performer (13).

The individual's general level of anxiety, as well as his needs for achievement, interact with competition to affect performance either negatively or positively.

Implications.   The boy who performs well in practice often does poorly when under the stress of the competitive game. When coaching gymnastics, the writer noted often that routines performed on the rings which emphasized strength were nearly always better under the stress of competition. Intricate routines performed on the high bar and side-horse, on the other hand, were frequently disrupted by competitive conditions. To counteract these disruptive effects, the writer frequently admonished the latter performers to "under-shoot" (reduce effort) in various tricks during meets so that these moves would be successfully accomplished under tension. The performances of people will change under competitive circumstances; those with high general levels of anxiety coupled with high needs for achievement will usually perform more poorly with the increased tension inherent in the competitive situation. Comparatively relaxed individuals who also have high needs for achievement will improve under competitive circumstances.

Assessing the effect of competition upon performance will be successful if the coach and physical educator take into account the nature of the task, the general level of anxiety the performer habitually evidences, his needs for achievement, and his prior exposures to the task under competitive circumstances. Competition will usually enable the performer to "learn himself," i.e., to become better able to predict performance changes which will occur when he is faced with the stress of competition, and to successfully adjust the effort he applies under these changing conditions. Practices which duplicate, as nearly as possible, the competitive circumstances which will confront the team on the day of the game should be successful in eliciting performance relatively unaffected by the actual adversaries. A more detailed analysis of the social implications of competition and cooperative behavior is found in Part Six (Chapter 18).

57.0 *Success is motivating; failure to do well is impeding to future performance (9).*

Although success and failure are subjective, some kind of judgment of this type is usually made by the performer (see Chapter 3, *Aspiration*). In general, success breeds success while failure breeds failure.

Implications. It would seem that, if the activity interest is to be kept at a high level, particularly with immature performers, initial success must precede the possibility of failure.

> **58.0** Environmental stresses such as extreme heat, cold, and noise are disruptive of performance, particularly performance involving complex perceptual judgments (10).

Implications. The physical educator and coach should pay as much attention to the control of these environmental factors as does the classroom teacher. Moderate cold and heat are often motivating; brisk weather seems to encourage vigorous movement, while a warm day often finds the athlete relaxed and performing well. If the athlete is subjected to environmental extremes, however, performance will be impeded.

One of the stressors over which the coach or physical educator has control is the sound of his own voice. Overuse of a whistle or overabundance of verbal directions can prove disruptive as continual blasts on an air horn in a factory. Current information theory emphasizes the importance of psychological "noise" in several forms as influential of the degree to which an individual can intercept and interpret incoming information. The coach and physical educator should be aware of the frequent need for silent trial and error practice of those working under their direction.

> **59.0** Fatigue can have a negative or positive effect upon complex performance (2).

In one frame of reference, fatigue has been paired with the concept of boredom, as opposed to tissue impairment, which denotes cellular changes attributable to prolonged exercise.

Implications. Although prolonged practice can have a detrimental effect upon performance (performance increments become less as a practice is engaged in), it has been recently shown that moderate fatigue produced by a task similar to bicycle riding had a positive effect upon complex performance involving hand-eye coordination.

Motor activity engaged in for a moderate period of time can frequently result in more relaxed performance, with resultant improvement in performance. Although it is usually demonstrated that a warm-up period prior to activity exerts no direct physiological effects upon subsequent performance, it is often indicated that prolonged warm-ups may have the effect of adjusting an individual's tension level to an optimum for performance of the task.

The effects of boredom and psychological fatigue can be seen as learning curves are plotted. The influence of massing as opposed to distributing practice, in an effort to dispel the negatively motivating effects of fatigue, is discussed in more detail in Chapter 12.

60.0 *Physical restriction can result in heightened levels of activity (15).*

Experiments in which animals are used as subjects indicate that, to a point, restriction of their movements results in heightened activity.

Implications. The writer recently observed an elementary school in which academic achievement was emphasized. Activities in the classroom frequently absorbed the children for the entire morning, without any break in the form of a recess. When these children were released from their classroom tasks at about noon, they went to the playground and spent the initial minutes there screaming with their heads thrown back and their mouths wide open.

Although there would seem to be an optimum amount of time in which children of various ages should be confined to a classroom environment and an optimum amount of time during which they should be permitted to engage in playground activities, there is little direct evidence relating to what this relationship might be.

It seems, however, that good planning on the part of elementary and secondary school administrators should permit a reasonable amount of outdoor activities interpolated between classroom periods that do not allow for extensive physical action. Prolonged confinement in classrooms may not heighten the need for physical activity, but may result in producing in the child an emotional or physiological state which is suppressive of physical output. Doing nothing physical may prove fatiguing, and thus have a negative effect upon subsequent performance. Activity has been demonstrated to reduce stress indices in the blood; blocking of this method of dissipating stress may, in itself, prove stressful.

61.0 *Positive instructions seem to have a more beneficial effect upon performance than negative instructions (16).*

Corollary 61.1   Positive rewards (e.g., praise) following completion of a task seem to have more benefit in the improvement of performance than negative reinforcements (16).

Corollary 61.2   Some studies with animals suggest that punishment is never effective in completely eliminating a response; only by failing to reward performance can a facet of animal behavior be eliminated.

Corollary 61.3   The quickest change in behavior can often be elicited when both punishment and rewards are used at appropriate times (1).

Implications. Although a more thorough discussion of the effects of instructions is found in Part Five, the physical educator should be aware that the nature of his instructions and the manner in which praise or admonishment is administered can have negative and positive effects upon the perfcrmance of children in his charge. For example, one study found that instructing a child to move his pencil down the middle of a groove had a more positive effect upon the accuracy of performance than suggesting he "avoid the edges" of the groove.

Corollary 61.4   Continual positive reinforcement while eliciting quickest performance increment could, if continued, result in a decrease in activity level of the individual.

Implications. While the coach and physical educator should be quick to praise superior performance and correct poor performance, if he continually praises and otherwise rewards students for average effort, his ability to change their performance will decrease with time. Research seems to indicate that *well-placed* praise and punishment in the form of social censure are more effective in motivating people to reach high performance levels, particularly during the later stages of learning a complex skill.

The teacher who continually praises is often looked upon as insensitive by his pupils, and as a person who does not really perceive the realities of the situation or the real quality or lack of it evidenced by performers in his charge. The well-placed praise of the strict, demanding teacher, on the other hand, is usually valued by members of a physical education class or of a team.

62.0   *Hypnotism has been shown to positively affect motor performance only within broad limits (12, 18).*

Although it has been advanced by some that hypnotism may be helpful in identifying and removing performance "blocks," the experimental evidence available indicates that performance in a hypnotic state is relatively unpredictable. Recent evidence suggests that people's needs to be controlled by others correlate highly with their susceptibility to hypnotism, and that many times individuals who act as though they are hypnotized are, in reality, engaging in a form of dependent behavior.

Corollary 62.1   Strength has been shown to be improved under the hypnotic state, while accurate, complex performance cannot usually be improved when the individual is under hypnosis (18).

Corollary 62.2   Steadiness has improved when it is suggested that the hypnotized subject "relax" (18).

Corollary 62.3   Endurance is improved when it is suggested by the hypnotist that his subject "will feel no pain" (18).

Corollary 62.4   Relaxation training, a kind of auto-suggestion, has been
found beneficial to the performance and learning of skills in which low tension
levels are desired, e.g., swimming (4).

Implications. Performance may be improved only in a general way
when individuals are hypnotized. For the coach or physical educator to
look to the hypnotist for a panacea to improve the performance of the
athlete does not seem realistic. In coach-athlete relationships, the coach
often seems to exert unusual amounts of control over his performers. At
times, this control appears similar to the relationship between the hypnotist and his subject. If we are to believe the literature concerning individual differences in suggestibility, it would seem that superior performance
might be elicited if the coach were sensitive to which boys in his charge
are highly dependent upon his direction and which are relatively self-
sufficient. The ethical implications of the foregoing are obvious. It is
desired that the performer become more self-sufficient rather than dependent as a result of his participation in athletics.

> **63.0**   *There are qualitative factors in tasks which make them in-
> trinsically interesting to the performer (5, 6).*

It has already been stated in the previous chapter that utilizing one's
capacities to the fullest is a motivating experience, at the same time that
the type of actions demanded by a given task further molds the motivational level of the individual. It has been found that manipulatory, exploratory, and other behavior which can only be described as satisfying
one's curiosity is highly motivating. But deeper examination of these performance characteristics leads to consideration of *what* it is about certain
tasks which encourages manipulatory and exploratory behavior. Why are
some tasks eagerly engaged in and others ignored, independent of extrin-
sic motivational conditions?

Corollary 63.1   Novel tasks are usually accorded more interest by primates
and children in experimental situations than are tasks with which the individual
has had past experience.

Corollary 63.2   The novel task may be a modification within a general
classification of tasks with which a performer has had prior experience (14).

Corollary 63.3   The novelty of the task may reside in the fact that it is completely different from any task with which the individual has been confronted in
the past (5, 11, 14, 19).

Implications. The importance of novelty has been demonstrated in
innumerable experiments with primates, children, and adult subjects. Yet

this principle is often ignored when devising physical education curriculums. Often, children confronted with the same task on the playground day after day devise their own variations to seek some measure of novelty where none has been provided by their mentors.

The situation must continually change if it is to elicit interest, and this change must occur more often when attempting to interest and motivate the immature. Continual exposure to a task results in habituation, decrease in motivation, and resulting decrease in inclination and capacity to perform. If this important finding is ignored by physical educators and coaches, they deserve the apathy with which they are frequently confronted.

The coach who presents a routinized series of practices for several months prior to the season would seem to be ignoring this important consideration. The writer has had personal success with presenting a new and varied workout daily to swimmers.

This seeking of novelty has had several theoretical explanations. One of the most satisfactory seems to be that humans seek an optimum level of complexity and satisfy this need by engaging in novel performance situations.

Corollary 63.4   A moderate amount of complexity is conducive to optimum attention and the inclination to perform many motor tasks. The "simple" skill is often ignored (19).

Implications. Frequent reference has been made to the fact that individuals prefer to be confronted with situations which offer them a challenge. The task perceived as too difficult will frequently be ignored, just as that perceived as not challenging enough. Not only should the teacher attempt to devise tasks and performance variations which are reasonably complex, he should also permit the athletes and children in his charge to invent and improvise variations to the situations presented.

Children will frequently evidence more vigorous and varied activity if permitted to explore their potential to move in situations which are relatively unstructured. For example, in a program administered by the writer, success has been achieved when, after a period of time during which the teacher has structured the situation quite rigidly, the children are requested to see "how many ways" they can jump over a rope, demonstrate their own ten ways of traversing a balance beam, and otherwise seek increasing levels of complexity.

> **64.0**   *The need to play seems as fundamental in humans as the seeking of food (6).*

It has been suggested that play is evidence of a mechanism which releases excess energy, and that it is a way for children to practice adult skills without excessive censure or fear of failure. Physical education programs do not need more subtle reasons for their existence than simply to satisfy this basic need.

Play is seen in animals, and between animals and man; play usually has definite time limits—a beginning and an end. There are usually some elements of surprise involved, and, in general, play seems to be a rather ubiquitous facet of human behavior. The interjection of play-like activities into otherwise oppressive practice sessions is frequently utilized by the more successful coaches in order to motivate individuals on swimming and track teams. Imitative games and other activities can be utilized with young children to teach swimming, encourage the development of such basic motor qualities as balance, and in other ways improve themselves in a number of desirable areas.

Summary

The foregoing discussion has only sampled the situations and activities which prove motivating to human beings. Motivation is related in direct ways to perception and learning. The manner in which we organize current experience, and interpret events and situations with which we are confronted, is partly dependent upon motives. At the same time, past experience molds both motives and interpretations of events. The statements contained within Parts Four and Five are frequently related to some of the concepts presented in the preceding pages. Separation of factors which influence performance, motivation, and learning by the experimental psychologists is artificial at best.

Consideration of human motives without discussing the social context in which performance takes place is also somewhat tenuous. Part Six, dealing with group interaction, holds many implications for physical educators and coaches who seek to elicit optimum performance from those in their charge.

It has been suggested that motives may be classified as those intrinsic to the task and those which are primarily dependent upon the social context. Motives may initially direct behavior by influencing the kind of activity an individual will select to perform; motives may be influential upon the intensity and effort put into an activity by the performer; and motives may be considered factors which influence the extent to which an activity is sustained. Investigations of human motivations will continue. It is believed that the principles stated above have summarized the highlights of current knowledge, and it is hoped they will stimulate productive discussions on the part of the readers.

BIBLIOGRAPHY

1. Allen, Sara. The effects of verbal reinforcement on children's performance as a function of type of task. *J. of Exp. Child Psychol.*, 1965, 13, 57–73.

2. Bartley, S. Howard, and Chute, Eloise. *Fatigue and impairment in man.* New York: McGraw-Hill, 1947.

3. Bendig, A. W. Factor analytic scales of need achievement. *J. of Gen. Psychol.*, 1964, 70, 59–67.

4. Benson, David. Effects of concomitant learning in relaxation and swimming on swimming improvement. Unpublished study, University of California, Los Angeles, 1958.

5. Berlyne, D. E. *Conflict, arousal and curiosity.* New York: McGraw-Hill, 1960.

6. Fowler, Harry. *Curiosity and exploratory behavior.* New York: Macmillan, 1965.

7. Gates, G. W., and Rissland, L. Q. The effect of encouragement and of discouragement upon performance. *J. Ed. Psychol.*, 1923, 14, 21–26.

8. Gould, Rosalind. Some sociological determinants of goal striving. *J. Soc. Psychol.*, 1941, 13, 461–473.

9. Locke, Edwin A. The relationship of task success to task liking and satisfaction. *J. Appl. Psychol.*, 1965, 5, 379–385.

10. Macworth, N. H. Researches on the measurement of human performance. Medical Research Council Special Report Series No. 268, London: His Majesty's Stationary Office, 1950.

11. Menzel, Emil W., Jr. Individual differences in the responsiveness of young chimpanzees to stimulus size and novelty. *Percept. and Mot. Skills*, 1962, 15, 127–134.

12. Moss, C. Scott. *Hypnosis in perspective.* New York: Macmillan, 1965.

13. Ryan, E. Dean. Competitive performance in relation to achievement, motivation, and anxiety. Paper presented to the National Convention of the American Assn. for Health, Physical Education, and Recreation, Minneapolis, Minnesota, 1961.

14. Sackett, Gene P. Manipulatory behavior in monkeys reared under different conditions of early stimulus variation. *Percept. and Mot. Skills*, 1965, 20, 985–988.

15. Shirley, M. M. Studies in activity II, activity rhythms, age and activity, activity after rest. *J. Comp. Psychol.*, 1928, 8, 159–186.

16. Strickland, Bonnie R., and Jenkins, Orvin. Simple motor performance under positive and negative approval motivation. *Percept. and Mot. Skills*, 1964, 19, 599–605.

17. Triplett, N. The dynamogenic factors in pace-making and competition. *Amer. J. Psychol.*, 1898, 9, 507–533.

18. Weitzenhoffer, Andre M. *Hypnotism: an objective study in suggestibility.* New York: Wiley, 1958.

19. Welker, W. I. Effects of age and experience on play and exploration of young chimpanzees. *J. Comp. Physiol. Psychol.*, 1956, 49, 223–234.

part four

PERCEPTION

Perception is a global term having many meanings dependent upon the orientation of the person using it. In the broad sense, perception is sometimes synonymous with intelligence and personality. In a narrower sense, perception has been aligned with a specific kind of sensory input—visual perception, auditory perception, kinesthetic perception. Perception is the process of organizing and giving meaning to experience. The specific components of the process, as well as the nature of the stimuli, tend to influence more exact interpretations of the term.

In past years, physical educators and researchers upon whom they depend have been primarily interested in physical output—counting pushups, agility, and other evidences of motoric competence. Recently, however, more experimental attention is being paid to the manner in which perception (input) influences output. Instead of being primarily concerned with how a child holds his hands when catching a ball, physical educators have become aware of the importance of effective visual tracking of the object to be intercepted.

Three basic classifications of information form the primary sources of perceptual modifications influencing the performance and learning of athletic skills: (*a*) perceptions related to movement, kinesthesis, and related tactile and vestibular information, (*b*) various components of visual perception, particularly perception of movement in space, and (*c*) perceptions related to the manner in which the individual rates his personal

9 Kinesthesis: The Perception of Movement

competency in physical skills. Perceptions related to this final category have been explored in the initial section of Chapter 3. This chapter will discuss some principles which relate to the perception of muscular movement; in Chapter 10, various principles related to the perception of stable and moving objects in visual space will be discussed.

Studies of perception and the perceptual process formed the beginnings of experimental psychology early in the last century. Consideration of the manner in which individuals think, see, and organize information gave impetus to investigations which resulted in the initial schisms between psychology and philosophy.

Perception and movement are difficult to separate as we gain information relative to components of the movement which influence subsequent components of the complex action. Movement itself results in information which we interpret and apply to movements which follow.

We rarely move without some degree of visual monitoring. As we learn, we begin to dispense with some of the necessity for close inspection, but young children and the elderly seem in great need for various pairings of the visual and motor systems.

Perception and the learning of skills are intimately related. Some authorities have suggested that all learning is perceptual change. As we learn skills, our perceptions of ourselves change, and these changes in judgment about our personal performance potential influence performance which follows.

On these pages, only a brief overview will be attempted, relating perception to athletic performance and to skilled gross movements of a variety of kinds. For more detailed consideration of some of these principles, the reader is referred to sources listed at the conclusion of each chapter.

65.0   *Kinesthetic perception involves the organization and interpretation of the speed, extent, and duration of movement (2, 12).*

Corollary 65.1   Perceptions based only upon information afforded by limb position are remarkably inaccurate. Little information is gained while holding an arm out to the side with the eyes closed (7).

Corollary 65.2   Measures of kinesthetic functioning are usually not highly correlated; various tests of kinesthesis seem to be measuring relatively specific attributes (2, 12).

To suggest that an individual has good kinesthetic sensitivity is an incomplete statement; one must specify the extent to which he performs well in what *test* of kinesthesis (e.g., in reproducing a limb position, duplicating a previous tension level, or making judgments about the speed of a movement). With some frequency the literature contains references to the possibilities of blindfolded practice of sports skills to heighten kinesthetic awareness and thus improve skill. There is little experimental evidence, however, verifying the value of such practice.

It is more practical and useful to increase the amount of visual attention given to a part of the body involved in a complex skill, with the eventual goal of removing some of the visual attention from the task. The child should be encouraged to watch his arm when throwing, and when kicking he should be asked to give close visual attention to the movements of the leg. Attempting to heighten the ability to perform skills through utilizing only the "kinesthetic sense" does not seem a very sound practice.

66.0   *Kinesthetic perception in certain tasks can be easily distorted by engaging in prior tasks (6).*

Corollary 66.1   The amount of distortion is dependent upon the intensity of the first task performed, how long it is performed, and how soon afterward the second task is engaged in (5).

The baseball player frequently swings two bats before coming to the plate—ostensibly to heighten a feeling of lightness in the single bat, and thus be able to swing faster. Jumping on a floor seems difficult just after leaving a trampoline. A light ball seems lighter just after using a heavier one. Indeed, in all cases where an overload has been removed, the perceptions of actions engaged in immediately afterward are frequently distorted.

Implications. Most recent research indicates that these modifications of feelings may not be accompanied by real, measurable performance changes. The "feelings" which have been changed are relatively transitory and quickly dissipated. To attempt to change performance in a real way through using, and then immediately removing, some kind of overload would not at this time seem worth the trouble. Unless the athlete is confronted immediately with the task in which improvement is hoped for, and unless the prior overload has been judiciously applied so as not to cause undue fatigue, even these subjective feelings will not be induced.

There are some indications, however, that throwing a light ball prior to handling a heavier one will aid accuracy. There seems to be a heightened sensitivity produced when children are asked to make the finer discriminations which transfers positively to handling balls of conventional weights.

67.0   *Kinesthetic functioning is closely related to the visual processes (15, 16).*

Corollary 67.1   Creating artificial muscular imbalances in the trunk muscu-
lature has been shown to distort visual judgments of the young child (16).

Corollary 67.2   Frequently, a kinesthetic factor is identified when contrasting tests of visual perception; this factor involves the apparent ability of the
subject to imagine himself moving within a visual presentation of some kind in
order to make better judgments about it, e.g., identify the right or left hand by
observing pictures of the hands in various positions (15).

Corollary 67.3   The sighted frequently tend to rely heavily upon visual
imagery when performing tasks blindfolded (4).

Corollary 67.4   Motor ability has been found to be distortable by delaying
the visual feedback occurring as a task is performed (14).

Corollary 67.5   Similar sized objects which are placed closer to a blindfolded subject are judged as larger than those further away, just as are similar
sized objects which are visually inspected (2).

Implications.   The "feel" of a movement and the manner in which it is
organized visually are interdependent. Attempting to separate visual from
motoric functioning may result in an artificial practice situation which may
be entirely different from the task it is desired to improve.

> **68.0**   *Scores on tests of kinesthesis have at times been shown to
> differentiate between athletes and non-athletes (12).*

Specifically, scores on tasks which require that the subject reproduce
various tension levels in the muscles have revealed slight differences between athletes and non-athletes.

Implications.   One of the most important components of vigorous
skilled activities is the reasonably exact duplication of force integrated
into the complex action from trial to trial. A tennis serve, kicking field
goals in football, and other kinds of tasks in athletics require that the
performer have an accurate perception of the amount of force required.

Recent findings suggest that the ability to reproduce various amounts of
tension in muscle groups (50-75 per cent maximum) is trainable, within
limits. Training programs which attempt to teach the athlete through
representations of the force patterns which should be used for a given
task (by inspecting spring scales, for example) might improve performance, particularly in tasks in which a controlled, forceful component
is important.

> **69.0**   *Information gained from sensory end organs which transmit
> information from the muscles, tendons, and joints is usually
> integrated with sensory information from other sources (e.g.,
> the vestibular apparatus, pressure, and other types of tac-
> tile cues) (8).*

Kinesthesis rarely operates without other kinds of sensory information integrated with it. Practice of movements designed solely to heighten kinesthetic sensitivity will be more successful if other kinds of activities are practiced, or if the whole complex activity desired to be learned is practiced.

Balance, for example, is closely related to stretch reflexes which are triggered by tension changes in postural muscles. Ability to integrate arm-leg movements is also important in balancing. The difficulty in balancing without vision illustrates the marked dependence balance has upon the stability of the visual field, and the importance of kinesthesis in balance.

The shape of a ball, as a total configuration, is perceived not only by movements of the fingers around its periphery but also by various cues gained from subcutaneous receptors in the palms and finger tips. Tactile training and the practice of activities which purport to heighten manual dexterity should thus contribute to the total functioning of the motoric system in human beings.

Tactile sensitivity can be improved through the application of several techniques. For example, a child might be asked to identify various objects, without seeing them, by inserting his hands in a box. He might be asked to identify an object with which he is familiar by finding its shape by feel within a box. Similarly, clay modeling and finger painting are ways in which tactile perception may be improved.

Manual dexterity can be improved by engaging in tasks which require some kind of steadiness-aiming component, such as attempting to place dots within small circles on a page, engaging in line drawing tasks emphasizing accuracy, and utilizing tasks requiring fine finger dexterity, e.g., placing pins in a box for speed.

These tasks can be made increasingly difficult by requiring more accurate performance, such as drawing a line between guidelines of decreasing width, requiring that the tasks be performed with greater speed, and/or requiring that the tasks be performed at the periphery of the child's desk, rather than in the central portion of his space field.

> **70.0** *Kinesthetic sensitivity is dependent upon the part of the "space-capsule" surrounding the individual in which the kinesthetic judgment is made (7, 14).*

Corollary 70.1   Limbs may be repositioned with more accuracy if the target position to be reproduced is to the front of the body at about shoulder level (7).

Corollary 70.2   Kinesthetic sensitivity with the arms at the sides of the body is less than when the arms are in front of the body (7).

Corollary 70.3   Early visual pairings of the hand-eye action system contribute to more accurate kinesthetic awareness in the space habitually utilized by the individual when engaging in tasks which require hand-eye coordination, e.g., the front from waist to shoulder height (16).

Implications. Clumsy children or others who have skill problems frequently lose awareness of the arm's position when drawing it back in a normal throwing pattern. The inability to visually inspect the arm as it is drawn out of the frontal space field and the individual's eyes are on a target may cause him to lose an awareness of the arm's location, cause him to drop the ball, or otherwise interfere with his skill. A child who throws in a restricted manner may thus be doing so not because of any inflexibility in his shoulder muscles, but merely because he wishes to retain visual contact with his limb as he draws his arm back.

Clumsy children may evidence a lack of awareness of their lower limbs when assuming positions in which the legs are not easily visually inspected, such as a pushup position. When running, these same children may have to watch their feet rather than their destination, a practice which frequently can result in inept performance.

When utilizing a ball in a basketball game, many inexperienced players will prefer to watch the ball rather than the court and their opponents. Some coaches, to counteract this, have placed shields under their players' eyes during practice to enhance the player's touch on the ball and train him to control it with his fingers independent of visual monitoring.

In all cases where the individual seems to perform in a relatively restricted amount of space, it is usually helpful to first pair vision with movement (request that he watch his arm being drawn back). After the movement has been integrated with vision for a period of time, it is a sound practice to again attempt to remove vision from its role in the task.

> **71.0**　　Measures of kinesthesis are influenced by a variety of conditions both internal and external to the individual from whom the measures are obtained (1, 3, 9, 13).

Corollary 71.1　　Fatigue generally decreases kinesthetic sensitivity (13).

Corollary 71.2　　The number of bodily joints involved in the movement influences perception of weights held (3).

Corollary 71.3　　The amount of the load upon the limb influences perception of its speed and judgments concerning duration of its movements (3).

Implications. Practice in sports skills in which it is desirable to heighten the feeling of the movements should take place, as nearly as possible, under the conditions which will be encountered in the real situation. Movements which involve handling heavy missiles, e.g., shot-put, if practiced without the load, will not usually contribute to the skilled output desired. If a task is performed under conditions which produce fatigue or tissue impairment, practice should duplicate these conditions.

Some feel that practice should initially require that the individual perform at the speed which will eventually be desired in the final performance of the movement. A more thorough discussion of the influence of initial emphasis on speed versus accuracy will be found in Chapter 11.

Corollary 71.4   Kinesthetic sensitivity to movement is generally more marked in the upper limbs than in the lower limbs (2).

Infants and children learn to control the movements of their arms prior to movements of their feet. Structure and weight of the upper limbs, of course, enable more finite coordinations than do the structure and location of the lower limbs.

Implications. It is suggested that, in many cases, skill must be "built from the ground up." Throwing movements may be easily acquired by the arms and hands, but integration with proper foot positioning and other bodily shifts accomplished through movements of the lower limbs may be more difficult to accomplish. Games and activities which emphasize accurate movements of the feet should contribute in a positive way to hand-eye coordinations in which the total body is involved.

The agility tasks generally valued by girls (hop-scotch, jump rope, and so on) probably prepare them better in basic movements than the activities prescribed by society for boys. Soccer and similar games played with the feet might precede the more complex games, such as baseball, involving hand-eye coordination.

72.0   *The speed with which kinesthetic perceptions may be formed during the execution of a fast movement suggests that our judgments of rapid, complex movements may be dependent upon the perception of a total pattern after the movement is made (17).*

Corollary 72.1   Divers and others about to perform rapid, complex movements which allow little time for conscious awareness of the component moves as they are executed sometimes spend time "thinking through" or "programming" the movement by silently or verbally practicing it prior to its performance.

Not only do our kinesthetic receptors afford us inaccurate information, but the information available is slow in being integrated. Input integration-output time is often slower than the time needed to execute such a complex sports skill as a batting swing in baseball.

The available evidence suggests that kinesthetic perception is of less value when the movement is practiced rapidly. The individual can only be aware of a complex pattern before or after the movement is made. Attempting to consciously organize kinesthetic input during the time in which many rapid movements are performed may impede their execution considerably.

If the coach or instructor emphasizes careful attention on the part of the performer to rapidly executed movements, he would seem to be courting disaster. The direction and spatial dimensions of the batter's swing in baseball are determined prior to his beginning the swing, just as is the pitcher's arm movement. These rapid movements cannot be readily altered during their execution. Learning these movements seems dependent primarily upon the individual's awareness of the amount of initial force they require, and practice in all their variations to account for all possible contingencies. For example, the batter should practice full swings designed to intercept low, high, inside, and outside pitches, as well as those "grooved" down the middle by the pitcher.

Summary

A considerable amount of research is currently being carried out to explore the nature of movement. Although many early psychologists formulated learning theories heavily dependent upon kinesthetic integration, a contemporary look at research dealing with the perception of movement suggests that kinesthesis is, most of the time, auxiliary to the important information fed in by the visual apparatus. Statements describing some of the current information related to visual perception are in Chapter 10.

BIBLIOGRAPHY

1. Cleghorn, T. E., and Darcus, H. D. The sensibility to passive movement of the human elbow joint. *Quart. J. Exp. Psychol.*, 1952, 4, 66–77.
2. Coan, Richard W. Factors in movement perception. *J. Consult. Psychol.*, 1964, 28, 384–402.
3. Comalli, Peter E., Jr., Wapner, Seymour, and Weiner, Heinz. Effect of muscular involvement on size perception. *Percept. and Mot. Skills*, 1959, 9, 116.
4. Cratty, Bryant J. Characteristics of human learning in a locomotor maze. *Calif. J. Ed. Res.*, 1962, 14, 36–42.

5. Cratty, Bryant J. Figural after-effects resulting from gross action patterns; the amount of exposure to the inspection task and the duration of the after-effects. *Res. Quart.*, 1965, 36, 237–245.

6. Cratty, Bryant J., and Hutton, Robert S. Figural after-effects resulting from gross action patterns. *Res. Quart.*, 1964, 35, 147–160.

7. Fitts, P. M., and Crammell, C. Location discrimination II, accuracy of reaching movements to 24 different areas. USAF Air Material Command Technical Report 5833, 1950.

8. Fleishman, Edwin A., and Rich, Simon. Role of kinesthetic and spatial-visual abilities in perceptual-motor learning. *J. Exp. Psychol.*, 1963, 66, 6–11.

9. Howard, I. P., and Templeton, W. B. *Human spatial orientation.* New York: John Wiley & Sons, Inc., 1966.

10. Laidlow, R. W., and Hamilton, M. A. A study of thresholds in appercep-tion of passive movement among normal subjects. *Bull. Neurol. Inst. New York*, 1937, 6, 268–273.

11. Lloyd, Andree J., and Caldwell, Lee S. Accuracy of active and passive posi-tioning of the leg on the basis of kinesthetic cues, *J. of Comp. and Physiol. Psychol.*, 1965, 60, 162–166.

12. Scott, Gladys M. Measurement of kinesthesis. *Res. Quart.*, 1955, 26, 324–341.

13. Slater-Hammel, A. Measurement of kinesthetic perception of muscular force with muscle potential charges. *Res. Quart.*, 1957, 28, 153–159.

14. Slocum, Helen M. The effect of fatigue induced by physical activity on certain tests in kinesthesis. *Diss. Ab.*, 1953, 13, 1084–1085.

15. Smith, Karl U., and Smith, William M. *Perception and motion.* Phila-delphia: W. B. Saunders Co., 1962.

16. Thurston, L. L. *Some primary abilities in visual thinking.* Chicago: Uni-versity of Chicago Psychometric Laboratory Report 59, 1950.

17. Wapner, Seymour, and Werner, Heinz. *Perceptual development, an investi-gation within the framework of sensory-tonic field theory.* New York: Clark University Press, 1957.

18. Wegner, M. A., Jones, F. N., and Jones, M. T. *Physiological psychology.* New York: Holt, 1956.

All observable movement may be described in spatial terms. The ability to perform sports skills effectively is often dependent upon the ability to make accurate judgments about the movements of objects in space. Analysis of a number of activities within the physical education curriculum makes it clear that many of them are heavily loaded with perceptual factors rather than motor factors, primarily those which involve catching, throwing, and striking balls.

A few years ago, the typical reaction of the coach observing a boy who appeared unable to catch a ball would have been to correct the manner in which he held his hands as he prepared for the ball's arrival. However, physical education instructors are coming to realize that the child's ability to visually track the ball, to anticipate the path of its trajectory, is as important as the motor acts of running to the approximate location and placement of hands when the ball arrives. Recent research has suggested that certain types of perceptual training may be useful in the improvement of activities which were previously considered primarily motor skills.

Underscoring the importance of the perceptual process in performance are frequent references in the literature to "perceptual-motor skill" rather than simply "motor skill." Experimentally, *input* has been continually demonstrated to be indivisible from *output* when performing many skills.

Experimentation relative to space perception may be

10 Visual-Space Perception

divided into several classifications. One is dependent upon the complexity of the space field considered. Some studies of this type have investigated principles which aid in explaining the manner in which individuals make judgments about two-dimensional space in which no movement is occurring. Various tests which involve picking out a simple figure from a complex background are examples of procedures attempting to study this component of visual perception.

Other investigations have explored movement in two-dimensional space. Various tracking studies using a moving dot which the subjects attempt to keep within the cross hairs of vertical and horizontal lines, which are manipulated by two knobs, are examples of studies in this second category.

Less frequent are studies which have attempted to ascertain the manner in which humans organize complex information occurring in a *three-dimensional and moving space field,* despite the fact that it is this kind of situation with which the sports performer is constantly confronted.

A recent survey of the various factorial studies of visual-space perception concluded that there are four primary attributes which human beings evidence when observing and reacting to various spatial problems: (*a*) the ability to structure the situation, to synthesize complex information, (*b*) the ability to select an object or objects out of space with which to deal in some way, (*c*) the ability to make judgments rapidly, "perceptual speed," and (*d*) the ability to make varied judgments, to evidence "perceptual flexibility" (2). Most of the perceptually "loaded" tasks on the athletic field evidence several of these attributes. For example, catching a ball involves the ability to select the ball out of a complex background as well as the ability to make this judgment with some speed.

When selecting the following statement for discussion, the writer did not attempt to cover comprehensively the vast experimental literature concerned with visual-space perception. The criterion for selection was its potential usefulness to the coach and physical educator.

73.0   Judgments about the movement and distance of objects in space are dependent upon the presence of other cues available (4, 8).

Corollary 73.1   In the absence of a sufficient number of cues between the observer and the moving object, forming judgments about the distance and movement of balls is extremely difficult (4).

Corollary 73.2   Objects which overlap other objects are perceived as closer. The observation of objects on a textured background, e.g., a lawn, aids in perceiving their distance (4).

Corollary 73.3   The presence of converging lines in the space field aids in the perception of distance and of movement of objects in space (8).

Spatial judgments about movement and distance are extremely difficult to make in the absence of auxiliary cues (when observing a ball overhead against a cloudless sky, when attempting to "dock" a space ship to a satellite vehicle, and similar situations).

Implications. It is clear that practice must precede a child or youth's being able to predict accurately the location and speed of a ball moving toward him. The statements above suggest that this practice might be more worthwhile if emphasis were placed upon situations in which more difficulty would be expected to occur (such as catching a high fly in baseball); at the same time, making the performer aware of some of the auxiliary cues available to him when attempting to intercept balls would prove helpful. Ball catching practice on a gridded field while keeping the ball low might assist a boy to organize his judgments of movement. Practice against a simple background might also facilitate a boy's initial efforts at catching.

> **74.0** The angle upon which a ball is moving toward the individual will influence the accuracy with which he can perceive its speed and the point at which he may intercept it. (11, 12).

Corollary 74.1 The speed of a ball thrown directly at the catcher will be more difficult to judge than will a ball thrown at an angle, and intersecting other spatial signposts as it arrives.

A recent investigation indicates that the ability to judge quickly the arrival point of a ball projected directly toward an individual is not fully developed in children until about the age of nine or ten (14).

> **75.0** The perception of movement in space is partly dependent upon the individual's ability to judge time intervals accurately (12, 13).

Corollary 75.1 Time intervals will frequently be misjudged, i.e., a short time will be perceived as longer, if an individual is highly motivated and/or emotionally tense (2).

Implications. To achieve the maximum benefit from practice with ball catching, hitting, and so on, the individual should be relatively relaxed and free from pressure to achieve. Muscular tension which may arise from emotional causes may not only make the hands less efficient when contacting the ball, but can also disrupt the individual's ability to track the ball accurately and predict the point on its trajectory at which he can successfully intercept it. Social pressure placed upon the boy with perceptual problems when he misses balls coming toward him will only heighten his ineptitude.

76.0   *The size of a missile influences judgments about its velocity; at the same time, the perceived velocity of a missile will often be dependent upon perceptions about its size, particularly in the absence of other cues (3, 13).*

Corollary 76.1   A smaller missile traveling at the same speed as a larger one will be perceived as moving faster.

Corollary 76.2   A smaller ball moving at a slower speed than a larger one will frequently be perceived as moving at the same velocity.

Corollary 76.3   A larger ball must be thrown faster than a smaller one to be perceived as moving at the same speed.

Implications. The necessity for confronting a child with balls of various sizes thrown from a variety of angles seems obvious. In a skills program conducted by the writer, the instructors will frequently play ball with a child using spheres of various sizes and weights, and interchange their use in an unpredictable manner. The child is thus required to become perceptually flexible and change his tracking and catching program frequently. Bringing to the child an awareness of these principles also seems important so that he will not tend to anticipate the arrival of a small ball too soon nor attempt to intercept a larger one too early.

77.0   *If one is confronted with several objects moving at the same time within the space field, the faster moving one will be selected for attention (7).*

We tend to be distracted by fast movement even though we may not intend to deal with the faster moving objects.

Corollary 77.1   If two objects are moving at the same time within the individual's space field, they will tend to affect the perceptions of the individual when they are nearest each other. When they are relatively far apart they will be organized independently and not prove mutually distorting.

For example, if two objects cross each other's pathways, immediately after the crossing occurs they will tend to mutually distort the individual's perceptions of their speeds.

Frequently, in sports situations, an individual has to deal with several moving objects at the same time and to select one for his attention. The shortstop, despite the presence of a base runner moving rapidly from left to right, must intercept the ball hit directly at him, in which there is little left-right movement. The quarterback in American football must locate the receivers despite the presence of an onrushing defensive lineman and the movement of defensive halfbacks.

In certain sports, this type of perceptual distortion is frequently exploited. The rapid hand movements of competitive wrestlers when facing each other, and of basketball players on defense, are probably intended to confuse their opponents.

Implications. Practice sessions should attempt, as nearly as possible, to incorporate *all* the moving background objects against which the performer must isolate a central figure when performing. Infield practice in baseball, without the presence of confusing base runners, might not assist the infielders in their perceptual task as much as is usually expected. Quarterbacks and others in whom the ability to remain relatively "distraction free" is important should be trained with distracting game conditions present, particularly those in which rapid movements extraneous to the main requirements of the task can be expected to disrupt performance. The distracting hand movements of defensive linemen and basketball players should be utilized in practice if it is expected that future opponents will engage in this kind of behavior.

78.0 *Measurable perceptual differences have been identified between athletes and non-athletes (10).*

Corollary 78.1 The eye movements of good batters tracking rapidly moving balls have been observed as "smoother" than the eye movements of poor athletes (6, 11).

Corollary 78.2 The speed with which perceptual judgments are made by athletes is faster than the perceptual speed of non-athletes (10).

Corollary 78.3 Peripheral vision in athletes has been shown to be superior to that of non-athletes (10, 12).

Corollary 78.4 Depth perception and the amount of information organized in a single visual fixation has been shown to be superior in athletes (12).

In general, the literature indicates that slight to moderate differences in perceptual ability can be detected between groups of superior athletes when compared with individuals who have not participated extensively in athletics.

Implications. Although it is difficult to determine whether perceptually superior people enter athletics or whether participation in certain sports enhances certain perceptual attributes, it would seem possible to improve the perceptual capacities of athletes in various ways. Several drills have attempted to improve the speed with which a quarterback can select an "open" and to whom to throw. These drills may involve positioning the athlete with his back to the complex movements of his teammate, and then asking for a quick turn and throw. With such practice, some have speculated, perceptual speed and selection may be improved. Reaction time to various complex perceptual events may be improved upon repeated exposure to the events.

Various screening tests might be administered to athletes which attempt to assess such perceptual capacities as peripheral vision. Most such screening tests utilized to select athletic teams in the past have emphasized motor rather than perceptual capacities. Although some investigations have indicated that specific perceptual attributes are found in individuals participating in various sports (e.g., superior basketball players seem to have good peripheral vision), there is not much valid evidence as to just *what* perceptual factors are important for people playing specific positions on different sports teams. Such a battery of perceptual tests should assess the different requirements of various kinds of games as well as the unique tasks of each team member.

Training tasks to improve perception have usually been found more influential of performance during the initial stages of learning rather than during the later stages of acquiring a perceptual-motor task. At the same time, many such training procedures can be utilized in connection with the motoric output required by the task.

79.0   *Perceptions of the distance, size, and velocity of objects are interrelated judgments (1, 5).*

Corollary 79.1   The more rapidly an object is seen to get larger when approaching, the faster it is perceived as traveling.

The speed of an object is based upon perceptual judgments of the time taken traveling a perceived distance.

Implications.   Some of the training procedures previously described are supported by the above statement. Perception of moving objects is a dynamic, complex process, and all the facets of the situation must be analyzed and taken into consideration if the training is to be successful. If the child seems to have trouble estimating velocity, it may prove helpful to hang a ball on a string, and swing it from left to right and from near to far while asking him to touch it with his finger.

If the child seems to have trouble adjusting quickly to the velocities of balls of various sizes, balls of a single size should be utilized first. It has frequently been found helpful to work with balls of two sizes when training children with perceptual-motor difficulties—a small one to be thrown and then rolled back to the child, and a larger one which the child can catch and then roll back to the instructor.

80.0   *Perceptions of the distance of moving objects improve if the objects are moving more rapidly, up to a point (1, 5).*

Implications. Children with skill problems must often be trained gradually to estimate the distances at which objects are placed while both they and the objects are relatively stable. However, difficulty is sometimes encountered if the objects are initially moved too slowly in such a training program. There seems to be an optimum rate of speed of objects which is organized best by children.

81.0   *When the observer, i.e., the catcher or thrower, is moving, the perceptual judgments required to intercept objects accurately become more complex (2).*

Our perceptions of moving objects are based upon judgments about personal positions in space. When one changes position, the perceived speed and direction of his movements must be integrated with information obtained from the visual space field prior to throwing to others or to anticipating the pathways of oncoming balls.

Implications. A running pass in football requires different and more complex perceptual organization from the thrower than a pass executed as the quarterback is fixed. Practice programs, of course, must be designed to take these differences into consideration.

82.0   *Balls in sports may at times approach or retreat too rapidly to be accurately tracked, taking into consideration the functional limitations of the visual system (12).*

Implications. Asking the performer to keep his eye on the ball should result in better performance, as at least he will not anticipate its interception by extraneous and undesired bodily movements. Research indicates that it becomes impossible at times for the visual tracking system to actually track missiles as they reach certain speeds in various sports situations.

83.0   *There are some indications that humans may track objects and judge the speed of objects better when they travel in some directions within their space field than when they move in others (1, 3, 5).*

Corollary 83.1   It has been suggested that humans make more accurate judgments when looking at ascending objects than when attempting to track descending objects (3, 5).

Corollary 83.2   The literature suggests that the speed of an object moving from left to right is as accurately judged as the speed of an object moving from right to left (5).

Implications. It is usually observed when working with children that great difficulty is often encountered when balls are thrown high in the air; at the same time, balls coming at the children from certain angles seem more difficult to catch than those thrown from other angles. It is apparent that children must be taught to organize balls as projected through a variety of pathways in their space field.

It is also believed important to make children aware of various physical properties of projected and free-falling objects. For example, calling the child's attention to the fact that a ball falls with increasing speed, and when hit high must be caught by stepping under it perhaps slightly before he thinks he should step under it, would seem to prove helpful. At all times the maturity of the child, as well as his ability to understand principles of this nature, must be kept in mind.

Summary

The information in this chapter and in Chapter 9 relates to perceptions based upon the characteristics of the space field and to judgments made about movements. In Chapter 11, statements are presented which relate to the perceptual process as it is influenced by objects, words, and events which are under the control of the teacher.

The separation of kinesthesis, vision, and instructions is artificial, and only necessary in fulfilling requirements of organization. Kinesthesis, balance, and vision, for example, are closely related. Implications for instructions and training cannot omit the importance of the visual demonstration and the film, both of which relate to the principles of visual-space perception. Many tests of so-called visual perception include a kinesthetic factor which involves the individual's ability to project himself into a picture or situation and through imagery manipulate, in some way, the figures present.

The foregoing statements do not present a simple picture, for the elements and judgments which hinge upon various characteristics of moving and stable spaces are extremely complex. Scholars are in awe of the complex judgments of which humans seem capable when moving in, reacting to, and otherwise dealing with rapidly moving balls in various sports situations.

Further research is needed on these problems. Relatively little evidence is currently available in many of the problem areas covered. For example, only recently has an investigation been carried out exploring the abilities of children of various ages to move and intercept balls. Despite these beginnings, we know relatively little concerning the worth of the training programs and techniques suggested on the previous pages.

BIBLIOGRAPHY

1. Brown, Robert H. Visual sensitivity to differences in velocity. *Psychol. Bull.,* 1961, 58, 89–101.

2. Cratty, Bryant J. *Movement behavior and motor learning,* Chap. 7, Perception and movement in extended space. Philadelphia: Lea & Febiger, 1967.

3. Gemelli, A. The visual perception of objective motion and subjective movement. *Psychol. Rev.,* 1954, 61, 302–314.

4. Gibson, J. J. *Perception of the visual world.* Boston: Houghton Mifflin, 1950.

5. Goldstein, Jacob, and Weiner, Charles. On some relations between the perception of depth and of movement. *J. of Psychol.,* 1963, 55, 3–23.

6. Hubbard, F., and Seng. C. N. Visual movements of batters. *Res. Quart.,* 1954, 25, 42–47.

7. Johannson, Gunnard. *Configurations in event perception.* Uppsala: University Press, 1950.

8. Liebowitz, H. W., and Lomont, J. F. *The effect of grid lines on the field of view upon perception of motion.* Technical Report #54-201, March, 1954, Wright-Patterson Air Force Base.

9. ————. *Visual perception.* New York: Macmillan, 1965.

10. Miller, Donna Mae. The relation between some visual perceptual factors and the degree of success realized by sports performers. Doctoral dissertation, University of Southern California, 1960.

11. Mott, Jane Adele. Eye movements during initial learning of motor skills. Doctoral dissertation, University of Southern California, 1954.

12. Olsen, E. A. Relationship between psychological capacities and success in college athletics. *Res. Quart.,* 1956, 27, 79–89.

13. Weber, C. O. The properties of space and time in kinesthetic field of force. *Am. J. Psychol.,* 1927, 38, 597–606.

14. Williams, Harriet H. The perception of the pathway of balls by elementary school children. Unpublished study, Perceptual-Motor Learning Laboratory, University of California at Los Angeles, 1966.

In addition to perceptions formed from movements and judgments which depend upon vision, the performer receives information from others. The athlete thus gains knowledge upon which to base future performance from a number of sources—the feel of his own movements, his perceptions of time and space in which he is moving and in which he may be observing objects move, and specific "feedback" offered by the coach or physical education teacher. From these sources of information, he forms decisions, i.e., gives instructions to himself, concerning whether he should act in the same manner as previously, modify his action, or completely cease activity.

Methods of learning may be placed on a scale—from practice dependent upon precise instructions to practice which is purely trial-and-error. The effective instructor is usually able to interject himself into the situation at opportune times, correct the performers' attempts, and not interfere with his athletes' efforts to integrate information and act upon it toward the end of the learning process.

Instructions can be viewed within several classification systems; some are instructions differing in the time during which they are interjected into the performance-learning situation, and others are instructions which differ according to the type of sensory input involved.

Thus the statements offered here overlap some of those previously made, particularly guidelines concerned with visual perception. Instructions may be

11 Instructions

verbal, may come in the form of some visual representation of the act (films, demonstrations), or may appear as the instructor attempts to move the performers' limbs in the desired movement patterns.

Instructions may also be divided into those offered prior to the task, those which accompany performance of the task, and information extended to the learner at the completion of the task.

The statements which follow attempt to guide the reader toward the consensus of experimental knowledge of the effect of instructions on performance. Perhaps in no other area has the physical educator been more remiss in producing research. The following principles should be read critically by the reader; they should be applied only upon exercising one's best judgment to evaluate the nature of the learner, the kind of task, and the characteristics of the situation in which the instructions are to be offered.

84.0   *Prior to starting an activity, the performer forms a "set" or attitude toward the task* (13).

Corollary 84.1   A portion of this "set" concerns the amount or intensity of the task and its possible duration (12).

This information can be withheld or given to the performer with varying degrees of accuracy by the instructor.

In general, athletes will tend to protect their physiological integrity by pacing themselves through a workout. The coach, on the other hand, usually attempts to encourage them to extend themselves, i.e., to "hurt" themselves by tolerating varying degrees of overload.

Implications. Although, at times, coaches have attempted to elicit harder work on the part of their athletes by withholding the nature of their practices—particularly in swimming and track workouts—the results have been disastrous. If the athlete does not know what the intensity of the workout will be, he will usually pace himself to a marked degree, performing at low levels initially and preparing himself for the most intense workout he can imagine. Although pacing to varying degrees will always be engaged in by individuals confronted with intense workouts, knowing the exact dimensions of the workout will result in significantly less of this. The coach and physical education instructor will be more successful in eliciting maximum effort, therefore, by outlining the exact dimensions of the efforts they expect within a given time period rather than by giving inexact, incorrect instructions or withholding information concerning the nature of the overload they intend to impose.

Corollary 84.2   Another portion of this "set" involves the performer's attempt to relate the task to be engaged in with others in which he has had experience (5, 10, 14).

Implications. The instructor should always attempt to aid the performer to "bridge" his past experience with the present activity requested. Informing the athlete of the task's relevance to the whole sport and/or its relationship to previously encountered sports skills will be productive. Scholars who have examined the characteristics of the learning curve have identified the quick initial increase in performance usually evidenced when learning a motor skill as the "discovery phase." This discovery by the learner of the relationship of his present task to ones with which he has had past experience will be quicker if the instructor attempts to aid him in drawing upon his past experience in meaningful ways.

> **85.0** There are individual differences related to the manner in which various kinds of sensory input are effectively utilized (4, 8, 11, 20).

Corollary 85.1   Some individuals have remarkable ability to organize visually presented information quickly (4).

Corollary 85.2   It has been suggested by some clinicians studying human performance that there are several ways of classifying people based upon the sensory information they tend to use when learning, e.g., those who utilize vision versus movement, and those who synthesize information versus those who seem to dissect or analyze the situation (4).

Corollary 85.3   The manner in which individuals organize various kinds of sensory input when learning is dependent upon the nature of the task and the amount of time they have practiced it (6).

Corollary 85.4   Recent evidence indicates that some individuals tend to block out incoming stimuli, and spend more time in action, while others are relatively immobile, spending more time taking in and interpreting sensory information.

Although there has been some interesting speculation about the importance of various kinds of sensory input to learning skills, the physical educator, when confronting a large group of youths in a class or on a team, is most helpful when he can employ effectively all kinds of communication—both verbal and visual—and engage in manual guidance when appropriate. In experiments carried out by the writer, it was found when subjects were questioned concerning whether they employed various kinds of sensory information that they usually reported that more than one type was used in various combinations. When the nature of the task was shifted slightly, the reports of the subjects similarly shifted, and there were usually no relationships between the two kinds of reports elicited on different tasks.

The most effective learners synthesize information from several sources —material gained visually, through verbal directions, as well as the instructions elicited by the nature of the task. To argue, therefore, that the physical educator does not have to be a good performer and has no obligation to demonstrate the activity would seem to result in the omission of an important channel through which he may communicate with his students —visual demonstration. At the same time, the effective coach should be verbal enough to explain clearly the fundamental principles underlying the activities he hopes to transmit to the individuals in his classes and on his teams.

86.0   *Formal instruction is best placed during the initial phase of the learning process. Trial and error learning is best engaged in by the learner after he has mastered the task to some degree (6, 7).*

Although tasks can be arranged on a scale from those best learned with instructions to those whose learning is more dependent upon trial and error on the part of the performer, it is usually more helpful to place what formal instructions may be called for during the initial portion of the learning process.

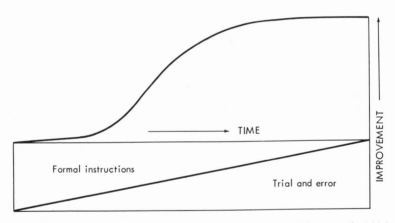

Fig. 4.   The Placement of Instructions during the Learning of a Skill. *During the initial stages of the learning process formal instructions are more important, whereas during the later stages, the performer may be allowed more opportunities to improve through exploring his own capabilities and assessing the affects of trial and error.*

Corollary 86.1   Mechanical principles related to the task are most effective when given initially; the spatial dimensions of the skill are also best transmitted early in the learning process (7).

The mechanical principles presented, of course, must be compatible with the level of understanding of the participants. Most new teachers and coaches attempt to re-teach the kinesiology course they have received as undergraduate teachers-in-training to the relatively unsophisticated secondary school youth with whom they are confronted—with the predictable results.

Corollary 86.2 Manual guidance is more effective during the initial stages of learning (14).

Factoral analyses of the learning of complex perceptual-motor skills indicate that perceptual factors are more prominent during the initial stages of learning, while motor factors (movement speed, reaction time, and so on) are more important during the later stages of learning. Initial instructions prevent the learner from adopting incorrect habits that might later have to be unlearned.

It is believed that the most effective coaches and instructors are those able to interject themselves at opportune times into the learning process. "Overcoaching" can prove as harmful as failure to offer properly spaced and appropriate directions. The performer seems to need information which enables him to *think* about the skill during his first exposure to the situation; later he seems to need to be left alone to permit various neurological mechanisms over which he has relatively little control to smooth and retain the coordinated act. The value of the opportune interjection of instructions has been demonstrated in investigations which follow longitudinal factoral analyses of skilled learning. After a skill has been analyzed, experimenters have interjected instructions or exhortations (e.g., move faster!) just before certain factors will become important in the learning process. Although sports skills have not been subjected to this kind of experimental analysis, the coach and physical education instructor should be sensitive to this principle.

87.0 *Knowledge of mechanical principles has been shown to enable the learner to vary his pattern of responding within the dimensions of a given task's requirements (5, 16).*

Many skills call for variations in the manner in which they are performed, thus it is imperative that an awareness is gained by the performer as to *why* movements in a complex act are executed in a specific manner. When offering information relative to mechanical principles underlying an act, care must be taken to consider the maturity of the learner and his ability to understand. In a skills program administered by the writer, some physical education majors have frequently had to be admonished for offering detailed kinesiological analyses of various skills to children classified as having mild to marked mental deficiencies!

On the other hand, children of junior high school age and older have been demonstrated to improve when offered mechanical analyses of various kinds prior to performing. Time-force graphs and more sophisticated information may often be presented with beneficial results to high school and college-age performers.

> **88.0**   *Visual demonstration is one of the most effective ways to enhance the learning of a motor skill* (12).

Corollary 88.1   The learner's ability to identify with the demonstrator is important if he is expected to duplicate his actions.

Implications. Observing an expert often has an *entertaining* but not an *educating* effect upon children and youth. If the learners feel that they are in some way comparable in ability, experience, or age to the individual performing the demonstration, they are more likely to attempt to duplicate his actions. Of course, the demonstration must be of reasonable quality if the actions are to be duplicated by the learner.

Usually the best approach is for a physical education instructor to select a student of medium ability from the class to perform the demonstration, one who will not fail in the new task and is not already perceived by the group members to be so superior that he cannot be copied. The rule for the instructor to follow relative to personal demonstration is that if he can perform an activity well, he should probably demonstrate occasionally. While demonstrations by the instructor-coach will perhaps enhance his rapport with his team or class, permitting class members to demonstrate with frequency should have a greater impact for the reasons mentioned above.

Corollary 88.2   Visual demonstration in the form of a film can be effective if practice is engaged in soon after the viewing (22).

The research indicates that verbal instruction accompanying the film should be well paced if the film is to enhance learning. If the time between the viewing and physical practice is short, learning will be further enhanced.

One of the most promising uses of visual cues in the learning of skills has been in the form of the videotape machine. Execution of physical activities in which severe spatial disorientation occurs (diving, gymnastic activities) has been found to benefit to a great degree from immediate videotape feedback. The performer receives vivid information relative to his performance. This is visual information which is unambiguous.

Verbal material is frequently subject to redundancy and ambiguity, while veiwing one's own just completed actions on a videotape represents one of the most dynamic new developments in the teaching of athletes. The team may view its recently completed play and correct itself immediately. The individual may observe defects in his performance and rectify them at once. One coach has interpolated a film of a model performance between the performances of members of his team. By comparing the two, the team members are able to correct their actions to match those of the expert demonstrator.

Another coach videotapes his games together with his comments, and replays the tape to his team immediately after the game. Some professional football teams will probably begin to replay the defensive sequences immediately following their execution, permitting the defensive team to view their errors while on the bench during the time the offensive team is on the field.

At times, however, various kinds of visual feedback may detract from skilled performance. A few years ago, the writer noticed that dancers were somewhat reluctant to perform in front of a TV camera videotape arrangement which enabled them to view themselves from behind while moving. A beginner whose movements are clumsy when attempting a new skill may not benefit from a more vivid awareness of the extent of his ineptitude via videotape feedback during the initial stages of learning.

It might be suggested that this kind of electronic equipment is impractically priced. However, as compared to the total cost of athletic facilities, it is relatively moderate in cost, keeping in mind the amount of individual and group improvement which should be forthcoming through its use. Vision is our most helpful sense; it is silent, takes up no room, and is capable of integrating complex information and providing aid with very little interference. Electronic developments which enable one to view oneself performing and immediately correct actions seem to hold great promise for the future.

89.0   *Whether emphasis is on speed or accuracy has been shown to be influential upon performance* (18).

Although some experimental evidence dictates that instructors should encourage initial practice at the speed the tasks finally require, recent observations of anthropologists relative to the manner in which primates instruct their young would seem to refute this contention. Tasks which are relatively dangerous or in which the individual's space field suffers some distortion, such as tumbling, seem to require initial practice at less than optimum speed.

Similarly, complex tasks involving several kinds of spatial integrations require initial practice at less than top speed. Recent experimental evidence indicates that when tasks are presented to children in which speed and accuracy are equally emphasized, children below the age of eight react only to the "speed stress," while at age nine, children attempting to integrate the accuracy components performed more slowly. By the age of ten, however, the children were able to integrate both the accuracy and speed components of the task into successful performance.

The maturity of the performer, as well as the nature of the task, would seem to dictate whether speed and/or accuracy are emphasized initially, and to what degree. Most of the available evidence indicates that in most complex and dangerous skills early speed is detrimental; understanding the spatial dimensions in which the individual must move are important initially; an increase in movement speed is more desirable toward the end of the learning period. Although some would argue that initial speed practice should duplicate final speed in motor tasks, the writer prefers to take his lead from the mother gorillas, many of whom have not had the opportunity to scan some of the "Principles" books in physical education.

90.0   *Emphasis upon what not to do versus what to do may adversely influence performance of skills* (17).

More success is seen, particularly in children, if performers are informed of the positive way in which they should perform, what *to* do, rather than being informed of what movements to avoid. One experimental task in which the subjects were informed that they should "move down the center of a groove," as opposed to being told to "avoid the sides," illustrates the relative influence of these two types of directions. Best performance, however, may usually be elicited if individuals are informed both of the things they should be attempting to do as well as the movements they should be avoiding. Learning a motor skill may be evidenced by elimination of errors as well as by increases in such positive aspects of the problem as increased speed.

Generally, this principle relates to the influence of negative versus positive reinforcement. As in the studies carried out with animals, quickest learning on the part of children and youth engaged in motor skills is usually evidenced when both negative and positive instructions are available to them.

91.0   *Manual guidance is sometimes effective during the learning of a motor skill* (14).

Manually guiding the movements of the learner is effective with individuals who seem relatively unable to profit from a verbal description of a visual demonstration. Children whose abilities to comprehend verbal directions are not highly developed may often be assisted to perform in this direct way. Individuals who have mild problems of visual perception are also amenable to manual guidance. Care must usually be taken by the instructor when assisting another to help him as little as possible, or the student's resistance to the instructor's guidance may actually result in muscles being activated which are inappropriate to the task.

Manual guidance is usually more effective during the initial stages of learning. During the final stages, as with other kinds of instructions, manual guidance should be utilized only to correct obvious deviations from the desired action patterns.

92.0   *Learning does not usually occur unless there is some way for the performer to obtain knowledge of his relative success or failure (1, 2, 9).*

Learning will be enhanced to the extent to which this knowledge of results is immediate and clear to the performer. The previous discussion of the use of videotape feedback is a clear example of application of this finding.

The performer will usually obtain some knowledge of his actions without the instructor. He will know if he is improving in accuracy, has gotten faster, or has become more skilled in other ways. For example, the writer compared the performance records of two groups in a large maze task, one of which received exact knowledge of decrements in traversal speed. When comparing the learning records of the two groups, it was found that there were no significant differences. The group which did not receive any information from the experimenter was still able to judge decrements in traversal speed accurately, and learned because of this perceived improvement.

Generally, spaced knowledge of results is not as effective as knowledge after each trial. The coach and physical educator should attempt to inform the athletes in his charge of their relative improvement, or lack of it, as often as possible and in terms they can understand. If we accept the previous statement that performance in itself is motivating, and that motivation results in performance improvement, accurate knowledge of the amount of improvement after each attempt should enhance performance dramatically.

It has been found recently that there is an optimum time after performance is completed that knowledge of results will result in the most improvement. A performer seems to have to have some time in which to consolidate the sensory information he receives from the skill itself, prior to being offered specific knowledge of his relative success or failure from an outside source.

Summary

Instructions prior to performance should outline the exact demands to be placed upon the individual in terms of intensity and duration. The task's mechanical principles and spatial dimensions should be clearly transmitted to the learner during the initial stages of the learning process. Verbal instructions should also be placed near the initial portion of the practice period; with increased practice, and as speed and accuracy are achieved, instructions should be extended less frequently. Toward the end of the learning process, the performer should be corrected intermittently, and should be permitted to experiment in a trial and error fashion with various modifications of the task's performance.

Strength and efficiency, as well as a decrease in errors, will result to the extent to which the performer receives accurate, frequent, and meaningful information relative to his success at duplicating the task's requirements. The performer usually attempts to integrate several kinds of sensory input at the same time. The sensory information important to the learner is unique to the individual, and shifts from task to task and from point to point in the learning process. The effective instructor and coach should prepare himself to transmit verbal direction well, present effective visual demonstrations, and manually guide his learners in an appropriate way and at appropriate times.

BIBLIOGRAPHY

1. Arps, G. F. Work with knowledge of results vs. work without knowledge of results. *Psychol. Monog.*, 1920, 28, 125.

2. Bilodeau, E. A., and Bilodeau, Ina McD. Variable frequency of knowledge of results and the learning of a simple skill. *J. Exp. Psychol.*, 1958, 55, 379–383.

3. Crafts, L. W., and Gilbert, R. W. The effect of knowledge of results on maze learning and retention. *J. Ed. Psychol.*, 1935, 26, 177–187.

4. Cratty, Bryant J. *Movement behavior and motor learning*. Philadelphia: Lea & Febiger, 1967.

5. Daughtrey, Greyson. The effects of kinesiological teaching on the performance of junior high school boys. *Res. Quart.*, 1945, 16, 26–33.

6. Fleishman, Edwin A. A comparative study of aptitude patterns in unskilled and skilled psychomotor performances. *J. Appl. Psychol.*, 1957, 41, 145–152.

7. ————, and Hempel, Walter E., Jr. Changes in factor structure of a complex psychomotor test as a function of practice. *Psychometrike*, 1954, 19, 239–252.

8. George, F. H. Errors of visual recognition. *J. Exp. Psychol.*, 1952, 43, 202–206.

9. Greenspoon, Joel, and Foreman, Sally. Effect of delay of knowledge of results on learning a motor task. *J. Exp. Psychol.*, 1956, 51, 226–228.

10. Hendrickson, G., and Schoreder, W. H. Transfer of training in learning to hit a submerged target. *J. Ed. Psychol.*, 1941, 32, 205–213.

11. Holzman, P. S., and Klein, G. S. Cognitive system principles of leveling and sharpening; individual differences in assimilation effects in visual time error. *J. Psychol.*, 1954, 37, 105–122.

12. Karlin, Lawrence, and Mortimer, Rudolph G. Effect of verbal, visual and auditory augmenting cues on learning a complex motor skill. *J. Exp. Psychol.*, 1963, 65, 75–79.

13. Katz, D. Gestalt laws of mental work. *Brit. J. Psychol.*, 1949, 39, 175–183.

14. Koch, H. L. The influence of mechanical guidance upon maze learning. *Psychol. Monog.*, 1923, 33, 147.

15. Lundgate, P. The effect of manual guidance upon maze learning. *Psychol. Monog.*, 1923, 33, 100–133.

16. Parker, James E., and Fleishman, Edwin A. Use of analytical information concerning task requirements to increase the effectiveness of skill training. *J. App. Psychol.*, 1961, 45, 295–302.

17. Silleck, Sidney B., Jr., and Lapha, C. W. The relative effectiveness of emphasis upon right and wrong responses in human maze learning. *J. Exp. Psychol.*, 1937, 20, 195–201.

18. Solley, William H. The effects of verbal instruction of speed and accuracy upon the learning of a motor skill. *Res. Quart.*, 1952, 23, 231, 240.

19. Wang, T. L. Influence of tuition in the acquisition of skill. *Psychol. Monog.*, 1925, 34, 154.

20. Witkin, H. A., and Asch, S. E. Studies in space orientation, IV, further experiments on perception of the upright with displaced visual fields. *J. Exp. Psychol.*, 1948, 38, 762–782.

21. Witkin, H. A., Lewis, H. B., Herzman, M., Mackover, K., Meissner, P. B., and Wapner, S. *Personality through perception.* New York: Harper, 1954.

22. Zuckerman, John V. Effects of variations in commentary upon the learning of perceptual-motor tasks from sound motion pictures. *The Amer. Psychol.*, 1950, 5, 363–364.

part five

LEARNING

Learning in the broadest sense is the organization of behavior according to the performance demands of some task. Operationally, learning has been defined as the stable performance changes caused by practice, as opposed to change elicited by drugs, nutrients, or some temporary motivational state. Learning a motor skill may be evidenced by decrease in errors, lowering of tension during performance, and general "smoothing" of performance.

Learning a perceptual-motor skill involves various adaptations by the performer to the demands of the task as he perceives them. It is dependent upon his interpretations of sensory information present in the total situation, including movement cues, visual feedback, and instructions from a coach or physical education teacher.

Learning is intimately related to motivation; it is often extremely difficult to separate the effects of learning from those imposed by varying degrees and types of motives. Perception is also closely connected with the learning process. The individual's perceptions of his own capabilities as they relate to his perceptions of the situation affect his initial effort as well as whether he attempts to learn a given task.

Evidence of learning is usually presented in the form of a "learning curve" which charts performance improvement or decrements over a period of time. Evaluation of the amount of learning taking place may then be carried out by subtracting the first from the

12 Learning to Execute a Perceptual-Motor Skill

final score, inspecting average improvement per trial, or measuring improvement after a few initial warm-up trials.

The improvement an individual will evidence is not always attributable to practice; in fact, it may be caused by no practice! The placement and length of the rest interval between practice bouts, whether the task is practiced as a whole or in parts, and what the performer engages in between trials are all influential of the learning of a motor skill (1).

The statements discussed in this chapter exclude specific reference to the variety of practice conditions which may influence learning; these are found in Chapter 13. In general, these statements relate to what is observable and measurable during a practice period in which improvement apparently takes place. The neurological underpinnings of retention and learning are little understood, and scholars in this area at the present time, are only able to offer various theoretical models to explain how internal biochemical and neurological mechanisms support the individual's outward change in behavior.

93.0 *Learning may be evidenced by both a decrease in errors and various measures of performance improvement* (17).

Corollary 93.1   Improvement in a motor skill may be evidenced both by increases in speed and in accuracy, depending upon the nature of the task.
Corollary 93.2   Errors of omission as well as of commission are eliminated during the learning of a motor skill. The learner is sometimes inaccurate because of an extra movement he interpolates into the skill, and at times he is inept because he fails to perform some component of the desired skill (8, 10).
Corollary 93.3   Perseverative errors are caused by interference in the complex response desired by a response from a prior act (10).

Implications. When teaching sports skills, it is important to be sensitive to the above statements. The performer should not only be informed as to the correct performance desired, but should also be aided to eliminate errors. The instructor should be particularly alert to the presence of undesirable components of the skilled response caused by prior performance of a similar but different skill. Further reference to the causes of negative transfer will be found in Chapter 14.

94.0 *Learning is usually enhanced by the presence of some kind of reward, either an obvious one or simply mastery of the task* (17).

Extensive reference has previously been made to motivation. In general, many learning theorists state that all learning is dependent upon some kind of reinforcement or reward. Extensive study has been carried out with laboratory animals concerning the effects of various reward schedules upon performance improvement. Other investigations indicate that, in the absence of reward, learning often takes place which is not recordable in performance improvement until the reward is suddenly reintroduced. This type of investigation indicates that the ability or potential to perform at a given level is often being improved, but is not evidenced until the proper rewarding conditions are introduced into the situation. Learning and performance are, at times, experimentally divisible. Learning is the result of long-term exposure to the task, and involves the ability to modify a response pattern. Performance, on the other hand, is rather short-term evidence of ability, and may or may not be truly indicative of the level of learning achieved by an individual.

95.0   *The shape of a motor learning curve is a function of the spacing of the trials, and of the capacities of the performer, as well as of the nature of the task (13, 17).*

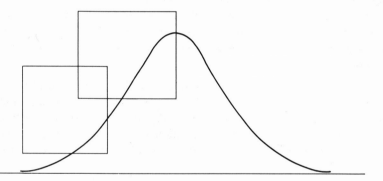

Fig. 5. The Learning Curve. *Some theorists have claimed that the complete learning curve resembles the curve of normal distribution. The shape of any performance curve recorded in an experiment, therefore, is dependent upon the point in the total learning of the skill which is being sampled.*

Corollary 95.1   Performance records of a task which is difficult or of a performer who is immature or whose nervous system is impaired in some way will generally produce a curve in which little initial improvement is evidenced.

Corollary 95.2   A capable and mature performer learning a task similar to those with which he has had experience will generally produce a learning curve in which quick initial improvement is evident, followed by a plateau effect.

Corollary 95.3   After an initial "discovery phase" marked by rapid improvement, there is a tendency for an individual to improve at a decreasing rate, and for the learning curve to register irregularities in improvement due to the imposition of various motivating conditions (16).

Implications. The inexperienced performer should often be expected to need prolonged practice prior to evidencing any measurable improvement. Undue pressure upon the performer during these exploratory stages in the learning process may only prolong this initial phase. On the other hand, the more experienced performer should be expected to improve rather rapidly initially, and the problem with such a performer is to overcome the plateau effect which he seems to reach at times. Suggestions for elevating plateaus in learning are discussed in this and subsequent chapters.

> **96.0** The learning process, relative to the acquisition of a motor skill, can be divided into several stages: preparation for performance, obtaining initial cues, gaining an understanding of the task, practice, and completion (17).

Corollary 96.1   All of these stages suggest different instructor-performer relationships relative to the quality and quantity of instruction offered.

Corollary 96.2   The learning of motor skills seems hastened if the performer is able to grasp an intellectual understanding of the nature of the task prior to beginning practice, and is given some time to himself in which to integrate the initial cues he may be perceiving from observing the task and listening to instructions (2, 7, 18).

Implications. The instructor and coach should be sensitive to the emergence of these stages in the learning process, all of which hold implications concerning the type and amount of instruction that should be interposed into the situation. A detailed discussion of instructions and learning was presented in the previous chapter, and will not be treated extensively here.

> **97.0** The initial portion of the learning process is more dependent upon perceptual processes, while the final portions of the learning of a motor skill involve more motor factors (7).

The implications for this statement were covered in Chapter 10, statements 76–80.

> **98.0** Plateaus, indicating periods of no improvement, may appear when plotting learning curves (13).

Corollary 98.1   These plateaus may occur because of fatigue or boredom on the part of the performer (13).

Corollary 98.2   Plateaus may be caused as slight changes in the task's requirements are made.

Corollary 98.3   Plateaus may be attributable to time needed by the performer to build up complex responses from simple ones (13).

If part learning is engaged in, a plateau indicating no improvement in the total skill may be evidenced as the performer integrates the parts into the whole.

Implications. One of the problems frequently plaguing coaches and physical educators is staleness in athletes; this is sometimes seen to occur near the middle or end of a sports season or school semester. The available evidence cited above indicates that these plateaus can occur for a variety of reasons. Their alleviation depends upon accurate assessment of the reasons and attempts to modify the practice environment to correct the condition.

For example, if it is decided that fatigue or boredom is accountable for periods of no improvement, the physical educator should lengthen the time between practice periods, allow more prolonged periods for rest, or otherwise modify practices to alleviate boredom. The interjection of rests during the middle of competitive track seasons is a means through which some successful coaches attempt to surmount the problem of performance plateaus.

Plateaus can also be evidenced when the performer takes time to build up complex response patterns from simple ones. This is seen clearly in the acquisition of typing skill, as the novice begins by learning responses to specific letters, later graduates into "thinking" a word and having a pre-set "program" for that word emerge through his finger tips, and finally attains the ability to type frequently used phrases with relatively little attention to individual words. The same phenomenon is sometimes seen in athletics, particularly among more immature performers in junior high school and high school. Attempting to master the fundamentals of the sport sometimes elicits learning plateaus of total skill patterns or team strategy built up from these skills. A coach who stresses fundamentals is often not too successful during the initial part of the season, but sees results of his work later, when the boys have had the opportunity to integrate the pieces successfully into the whole team effort. More specific implications for whole versus part learning are outlined in Chapter 13.

Slight modifications of the demands made of the learner may also cause either a performance decrement or a plateau in performance. It is surprising how specific the learning of perceptual-motor skills will sometimes be. In some maze studies conducted by the writer, it was noted that a short portion of the 50 yard long pathway composed of plastic tubing was sometimes amiss. This defect would be corrected as an individual was learning to move blindfolded through the apparatus. The adjustment would often consist of merely moving the railing at one point up or down an inch or two. When the performers reached that point in the maze, their hands would frequently slip off the railing. They had not only been memorizing the specific pattern required by the total pathway, but had unconsciously acquired the necessary up and down movements of the hands when guiding themselves through the apparatus.

The coach and physical educator should be aware of the possible negative effects of inducing slight changes into team and individual skills during the learning of a sport. Even slight variations in skill patterns or performance of integrated efforts will often result in decrements or, at best, in a period of time during which no improvement in the total task will transpire.

> **99.0** *A skill may be improved for a prolonged period of time with the proper practice schedule and proper learning (3, 10).*

Corollary 99.1 Improvement can be noted by observable changes in performance and also by less obvious indices, i.e., unconscious integration of respiration to elicit greater accuracy, the manner in which ocular movements are involved in the task, and similar subtle physiological and postural adjustments (8, 15, 19).

Corollary 99.2 Learning is governed at the higher levels of performance by certain limitations of response mechanisms (9, 10, 20).

Corollary 99.3 There seem to be certain inherent skill capacities which can be "triggered" to emerge, and individual differences in skill are explainable by reference to these basic differences in neural makeup (9).

Implications. Although it is apparent that, with prolonged practice under proper conditions individuals are able to raise performance to levels previously not believed possible, to suggest that top level performance can be achieved by *everyone* with proper practice is absurd. There are basic genetic mechanisms which control the utilization of nutrients and dispelling of wastes during vigorous exercise, and which result in individual differences in the ability to perform endurance tasks.

There are also individual differences in the ability to acquire skill quickly and accurately which cannot be explained by environmental factors. We cannot all be a Heifitz, nor can we all run a mile under 3:55. The coach and physical education instructor frequently train a group for strength-endurance skill feat employing similar training stress for all members, but they continue to evidence marked individual differences.

Frequently the coach responds by remarking that individual differences he observes at the completion of such a regimen are due to some character deficiencies on the part of certain individuals. He may suggest that such differences result because individuals "goof off," "have no guts," or similar charges suggesting that the boy is simply not trying or is in some other way thwarting the physical educator or coach despite the best efforts of the latter.

For years, educators have paid verbal homage to the concept that an individual's intellectual and motor performance is influenced by both environment and heredity. However, most educators tacitly tell themselves that *they* are capable of changing *anyone*, that they can enable *everyone* to perform at high levels if given the chance and if given individuals who have enough character to withstand long and difficult practice sessions. Recent evidence from the laboratory of the biochemist and geneticist suggests that this is simply not true.

The most helpful course of action for the coach and physical educator is to be sensitive to the type and amount of practice afforded those in their charge, and to attempt to elicit superior, skilled output by attending to subtle changes necessary in many tasks, e.g., the amount and placement of vision in movement and adjustments in the breathing cycle. At the same time, the instructor should be aware that, genetically, all the boys in his charge are not equal, and individuals will perform at different levels despite their application to the task and despite the best or poorest efforts expended by the coach and the performer.

> **100.0**   *Forgetting begins to occur immediately after the conclusion of the task. The greatest amount of forgetting begins immediately after the task is discontinued (2, 3, 8).*

Corollary 100.1   In animal experimentation it has been proved conclusively that there are short-, medium-, and long-term memory mechanisms operative in in the nervous system (9, 12).

Corollary 100.2   After a period of time, the amount of forgetting does not increase further but tends to remain constant (17).

Corollary 100.3   Retention of a motor skill is likely to be greater if the individual is informed, prior to the learning process, that the skill is to be retested at a later date (15).

Implications. To facilitate retention, it has been suggested that repeated practice be engaged in before the forgetting curve reaches too low a point. It seems best for humans to overlearn a task in order to facilitate retention and impede forgetting. There is an optimum amount of overlearning, usually set at about 150 per cent of some learning criterion, which produces the best retention over a time interval.

Although definitive research as to whether there is a long-, medium-, and short-term memory for motor activities within the human nervous system is proceeding, we are all aware of things we can remember today, of occurrences which we will have forgotten in a year, and of events and facts which we will probably never forget.

Many rhythmic, integrated skills, such as swimming and bicycle riding, are unlikely to be forgotten. Similar to freely flowing prose and poetry, many motor skills, because of their integrated nature, seem remarkably resistant to forgetting.

The physical educator and coach should encourage more practice in a skill which has to be performed in relation to changes in the situation which are not predictable or logical. These are the most likely to be forgotten after a period of no practice.

The available research evidence also indicates that, if an individual knows he will be asked to reperform a motor skill at a later date, he will not only learn the skill more thoroughly, but will retain the skill to a greater degree. Individuals seem to have to be "set" to retain skills; if a performer is unaware that he will be responsible for a demonstration of his ability to retain a motor task, he will not learn it as thoroughly nor will he be able to demonstrate the same degree of retention as an individual who has been informed he should retain the skill.

> **101.0**   The rapidity with which an individual learns one task is not usually predictive of the speed with which he will learn a second (11).

Corollary 101.1   Motor educability is specific, not general. Improvement in a skill is a function of the amount of practice in the skill, not of some inherent ability of people to learn (11).
Corollary 101.2   General factors underlying the ability to learn several skills include need for achievement, typical level of arousal, and ability to control tension level, as well as needs for social approval (6).

It has been suggested that the apparent ability of an individual to perform well in a number of skills and to learn them quickly stems from the strong need in some people to receive recognition, and their willingness to expend periods of practice in excess of the time others will spend.

Confronting people with a number of skills to be learned which are relatively unfamiliar to them, usually in an experimental situation, and then correlating the amounts of improvement, results in few relationships being demonstrated. While there is a tendency for individuals to learn how to learn (to generalize to some extent from one task to another), and to learn how to learn a given classification of tasks, under strict experimental conditions a general factor of motor educability is not usually identified.

> **102.0**   Cortical activity seems to underlie the continued performance of all skilled movements (20).

Neurologists in the nineteenth century suggested that, with the acquisition of skill, movements were progressively integrated at lower levels of the nervous system. However, with the advent of more exact metering apparatus, it has been found that complex, voluntary movements performed continuously are always integrated by the higher brain centers, even though in appearance they become reflexive in nature. Even balance, largely thought to be the exclusive control of the low centers of the brain, is actually mediated to some degree by the cortex.

Implications. The statement above suggests the need for thinking about the task prior to its performance. A "cortical program" seems necessary to provide a base from which observable movements may be improved in complexity, speed, and in the correct application of force.

Summary

Learning involves subtle adjustments of the physiological and performance capacities of an individual to the exact demands of a task. It is evidenced by performance changes, and by less obvious changes in the performer.

Learning may be evidenced directly through the measurement of performance increments and decrements. Indirect evidence of learning may be noted when various rewards are withheld for a period of time and then reintroduced into the performance situation.

Learning is a function of the nature of the task, the response capacities of the individual, and the environment provided by the teacher. In Chapter 11, principles related to the perception of instructions were presented. Chapter 13 discusses the manner in which practice conditions may be manipulated by the instructor-coach through the timing of trials, by adjusting the amount of the task practiced at one time, and by manipulating the kinds of things a learner is encouraged to do between practice periods.

BIBLIOGRAPHY

1. Ammons, Robert. Acquisition of motor skill: III, effects of initially distributed practice on rotary pursuit performance. *J. Exp. Psychol.*, 1950, 40, 777.

2. Bolideau, Edward A., and Levy, Michael. Long-term memory as a function of retention time and other conditions of training. *Psychol. Rev.*, 1964, 71, 27–41.

3. Bolideau, Edward A., Jones, Marshall B., and Levy, Michael. Long-term memory as a function of retention time and repeated recalling. *J. Exp. Psychol.*, 1964, 67, 303–309.

4. Bolideau, Edward A. (ed.). *Acquisition of skill.* New York: Academic Press, 1966.

5. Cratty, Bryant J. *Movement behavior and motor learning.* Chap. 11, Motor learning. Philadelphia: Lea & Febiger, 1964.

6. ———. A three level theory of perceptual-motor behavior. *Quest,* 1966, 6, 3–10.

7. Fleishman, Edwin A., and Rich, Simon. Role of kinesthetic and spatial-visual abilities in perceptual-motor learning. *J. of Exp. Psychol.*, 1963, 66, 6–11.

8. Fuchs, Alfred H. The progression-regression hypothesis in perceptual-motor skill learning. *J. Exp. Psychol.*, 1962, 63, 177–182.

9. Gaito, John, and Zavala, Albert. Neurochemistry and learning. *Psychol. Bull.*, 1964, 61, 45–62.

10. Garvey, W. D., and Mitnick, L. L. An analysis of tracking behavior in terms of lead-lag errors. *J. Exp. Psychol.*, 1957, 53, 373–378.

11. Gire, Eugenia, and Espenschade, Anna. Relation between measures of motor educability and learning of specific motor skills. *Res. Quart.*, 1942, 13, 41–56.

12. Glickman, Stephen E. Preservative neural processes and consolidation of the memory trace. *Psychol. Bull.*, 1961, 58, 218–233.

13. Kao, Dji-Lih. Plateaus and the curve of learning in motor skill. *Psychol. Monog.*, 1937, 49, 1–81.

14. Knapp, B. *Skill in sport.* London: Routledge and Kegan Paul, 1963.

15. Lavery, J. J. Retention of a skill following training with and without instructions to retain. *P. and Mot. Skills,* 1964, 18, 275–281.

16. McGraw, L. W. Comparative analysis of methods of scoring tests of motor learning. *Res. Quart.*, 1955, 26, 440–453.

17. Melton, Arthur W. (ed.). *Categories of human learning.* New York: Academic Press, 1964.

18. Naylor, James C., and Briggs, George E. Effect of rehearsal of temporal and spatial aspects on the long-term retention of a procedural skill. *J. of Appl. Psychol.*, 1963, 4, 120–126.

19. ———. Long-term retention of learned skills, a review of the literature. *Laboratory of Aviation Psychology,* Ohio State University and Ohio State University Research Foundation, August, 1961.

20. Paillard, Jacques. The patterning of skill movements. Chap. 76 in *The handbook of physiology,* Section I, Neurophysiology, 3, John Field (ed.). Washington, D.C.: American Physiological Society, 1960.

An important classification of variables influencing learning consists of the several ways in which practice may be conducted. The order in which various components of a task are practiced, how much of a task is practiced at a time, as well as whether practice is massed or there are relatively long intervals of time between practice sessions, affects performance and retention of perceptual-motor skills.

Auxiliary to these variables are the kinds of activities the performer engages in *between* practice trials of a skill. He may mentally rehearse the task or engage in another task. Whatever he does influences in some way his subsequent performance of the initial activity attempted.

When writing a previous text, the author discovered about 400 research studies dealing with the effects of massing and distributing practice upon learning. Studies of mental practice, although not as numerous, have begun to proliferate within recent years. Whole versus part learning, which seemed to interest educational psychologists several years ago, has not been researched with the same frequency during the last several years, but information from prior investigations provides some insight into problems of interest to physical educators. Investigations of the manner in which placement of a task in a series of other tasks affects learning were initially carried out with word lists composed of nonsense syllables. Relatively few investigations have studied serial order as influential of learning and retention of motor skills.

13 Practice

The statements which follow are based upon evidence gained from the investigations described above. Many times, the findings are contradictory, and are dependent upon the nature of the task. Some of these principles are interdependent; for example, whether massing or distributing helps learning depends upon whether the massed practice has been with a portion of the task or with its entirety. "Part practice" seems more helpful than whole practice when the task requires complex interactions with another individual.

At the same time, there are valid generalities which may be drawn from this kind of experimental literature. These generalities form the bases of the statements which follow.

103.0 *Massed practice is effective when the task is highly motivating. Spaced practice is best when the task is difficult, physically taxing, or relatively uninteresting to the learner (1, 6, 9).*

Corollary 103.1   As practice in a task continues, the interest of the learner may change, thus necessitating a change in the pacing of practice (15).

Corollary 103.2   With continued massed practice, improvement may become less with each successive trial (9).

Corollary 103.3   Progressively distributing practice more and more as learning takes place is often productive of high final performance levels (1, 6, 14).

Corollary 103.4   More important than the amount of rest between trials is the ratio between the amount of time taken to perform the task and the duration of subsequent rest. Tasks whose practice sessions last for longer periods of time are learned best if the rest period following practice is similarly extended.

Massed practice means practice trials in a task or its components between which little or no time is permitted for rest. Distributed practice means that a comparatively long period of rest time is permitted between trials.

Distributed practice is usually more productive of high levels of learning than massed practice. Many hypotheses have been advanced to explain this. Some have suggested that only the incorrect parts of the response will be forgotten between trials. Others have said that, as practice of a task is continued, one begins to learn, but at the same time a resistance to the task builds up which results in a plateau in the learning curve. To dissipate this resistance to the performance of the task, it has been further suggested that practice be spaced during the later stages of learning. One neurological model has recently been constructed to explain the effects of distributed practice upon learning. It is suggested that the everpresent random electric activity of the brain follows pathways of least resistance, i.e., those which have been faintly established by brief practice. Thus, during rest periods in which the organism does not obviously move, learning is enhanced by this neurological activity which "stamps in" desired neural connections.

Implications. From a practical standpoint, the teacher or coach should monitor carefully signs of fatigue and/or boredom as the individual engages in practice, and begin to distribute practice when these signs result in performance decrements.

At the same time, since achievement seems motivating, quicker achievement is forthcoming when practice is massed, particularly during the initial stages of learning. There is nothing more frustrating to many students in physical education classes than to be exposed briefly to several kinds of activities in "introductory" courses, and then not be allowed to continue practice and achieve proficiency. If initial massing results in quicker motivating achievement, practice sessions of an interesting task should be placed relatively close together.

Massing or distributing practice is not a function of program scheduling. The instructor has a choice within each class period of whether to mass or distribute practice of a given skill. The skill may be practiced many times during the period or, after some brief attention, may be discontinued to be resumed at another time during the period or later in the semester.

Similarly, recognition by the teacher of the concept of work-rest ratio is important. Skills practiced for extended periods of time should be followed by rest periods of longer duration than are tasks practiced for shorter periods of time.

A survey of the literature suggests that the soundest procedure to follow is to mass practice initially and observe the amount of progress. When improvement begins to suffer, practice should be distributed by permitting longer periods of rest between exposures. A successful adaptation of this method has been termed the *additive method,* in which progressively longer periods of rest are introduced between the trials as learning progresses.

Motivation and the manner in which skills should be practiced are interrelated. Practice may be massed in tasks which are highly motivating. Some authorities have suggested that motivation may be best evaluated by measuring improvement in tasks with various amounts of rest interposed between their trials.

Corollary 103.5   Massing or distributing practice usually has little effect upon retention (16).

Long-term retention of skill is influenced primarily by the performance levels reached initially, not by the practice schedule adopted for this initial learning.

Corollary 103.6   Massed practice may facilitate part learning if the learning of the parts is massed (14).

Under proper motivating conditions, a difficult task may often be divided into parts. It is often found that massed practice of the parts positively influences learning as they are synthesized into the whole complex movement. The statement which follows further explores part versus whole practice.

104.0   Whole learning is quicker.

"Wholeness" is a subjective term, and relates to the amount of the task a learner can effectively organize motorically and perceptually. In tasks which are not complex, mature learners will usually learn more rapidly if they are exposed to the entire task; time is needed to link parts effectively to the whole.

Corollary 104.1   Part practice is better if the learner is immature and/or the task complex. However, pure part practice is seldom engaged in.

Corollary 104.2   Whether a task has been learned in parts or as a whole is not influential of long-term retention.

Corollary 104.3   Progressive-part practice is seen more often than part practice. In this approach to learning, a part is learned, paired with a second part, and the two practiced together. Then a third part is practiced and the three parts practiced as a whole, until the entire task has been constructed (14).

The complexity of a task is the criterion for deciding whether it should be presented to students as a whole or in parts, and its complexity is partly a function of the complexity of the student. For example, walking is a complex act for a 21 month old child, while to one of three or four years it is not. Retarded children learn best when complex tasks are presented to them in parts rather than as confusing wholes.

The coach or teacher should teach as much of the whole task as possible, taking into consideration the complexity of the task and the capabilities of the learners in his charge. Attempting to stretch the ability of the immature, incapable, or inept child too far is an unsound procedure. The progressive-part method outlined above, in which parts are combined into wholes, seems the best approach for the child with learning problems.

105.0   Activity, or lack of it, interjected between trials of a motor task influences performing increments (12).

Corollary 105.1   Mental rehearsal of the task will positively influence learning, particularly when combined with actual physical practice (18).

Corollary 105.2   Mental rehearsal alone will not aid performance and learning more than physical practice (5).
Corollary 105.3   The positive effects of mental rehearsal are not influenced by slight differences in the intelligence of the learners (17).
Corollary 105.4   Mental practice is not influential of performance change in tasks requiring endurance (2, 18).

Research with mental practice indicates there are significant differences in performance between groups who are requested to "think about" or in other ways encouraged to rehearse the task without actually moving versus those not requested to do so. There is great difficulty, of course, determining *what* the subjects really think about, whether they attend to the task at all, and what kind of imagery they engage in—do they think about verbal descriptions of a task, imagine themselves doing it, or imagine a visual demonstration? Investigations have also demonstrated, with the help of sensitive metering equipment, that thinking about a movement will result in finite muscular activity in the muscles which control the imagined activity.

Implications.   The implications of the above statement and its corollaries seem obvious. Focusing class attention on the task and upon other class members' performance should help learning and performance. Thinking through a movement prior to its initial performance and between trials should also facilitate learning.

This kind of mental practice has been particularly helpful in gymnastic skills. Similarly, in skills which involve striking balls, mental practice combined with physical practice has been demonstrated to improve performance significantly. Mental practice has had little effect upon group performance in which complex team patterns are to be acquired.

106.0   *The intensity of the activity engaged in between trials is influential of performance* (12).

Detrimental effects are usually noted if activities between trials are intense, fatiguing, or similar to the activity in which improvement is desired. The best effects upon learning are gained if the activities between trials are mental practice or simple rest.

One widely accepted hypothesis to explain forgetting rests upon the concept that forgetting is elicited by interfering activities, rather than simply through dissipation of a memory trace. Within this context, it has been explained that the reason verbal information is so easily forgotten is that most individuals are continually bombarded with other verbal information which interferes with that information to be retained. In any case, the physical educator should be extremely cautious when interpolating activities between those skills which he hopes his charges will be capable of reperforming.

Implications. The coach and physical education teacher should place activities which are not fatiguing or otherwise taxing upon the intellect or physique of his class members between trials of activities in which improvement is desired. If activities between trials are similar to but not exactly like those of the reference skill, detrimental effects upon the learning of the latter will usually be evidenced. Further comments relating to positive and negative transfer are found in Chapter 14.

> **107.0** *The placement of a skill in a series of skills will influence its acquisition and retention (3).*

Corollary 107.1   Skills in the initial part of a series will be learned first and retained best (3).

Corollary 107.2   Skills in the middle portion of a series will be learned last and retained least (3).

Corollary 107.3   Skills in the final portion of a series will be retained better than those placed in the middle and not as well as those placed near the initial portion of the series.

Corollary 107.4   When learning a complex skill consisting of a number of parts, the components presented first will be learned quickest (3).

Implications. These corollaries have implications for placement of a skill within a single practice period as well as for organization of the school program. In general, the learning of skills near the beginning of a series is not interfered with by other similar activities. With continued exposure to a number of tasks, however, the individual simply cannot hold on to too many instructions and skills at the same time. The skills placed near the end of a series, i.e., near the end of a class period or toward the end of a school semester, are likely to be retained better than those presented near the middle. The ending of a practice session has a delineating effect, and makes the final skills stand out from those which went before.

Instructors in physical education should thus review skills which may have been presented during the middle of a class period or toward the middle of a school semester. Skills believed more important should be placed in positions which enhance their learning. The most difficult skills to be learned should not only be frequently reviewed, but placed within sports practice at times which encourage their retention and learning. A number of skills presented at the same time may tend to obliterate each other in the learner's mind. Judicious placement, as well as spacing of skills, are important considerations when hoping to encourage high levels of skill and good retention.

108.0 *Components of a skill whose learning has been interrupted are more likely to be retained than are components of a skill in which practice has been completed when it has been learned to some established criterion (4).*

Generally, the effect of greater retention because of interrupted practice is caused by the heightened tension level experienced towards the end of learning a task to a given criterion. This heightened general tension or concern about the task results in greater retention than of a task whose learning schedule has been completed.

Implications. In some cases, interest in a task or a group of skills may be heightened if the athletes or class members are left with questions at the end of a period, or are permitted to explore a new task briefly just prior to the end of a period. This brief exposure should serve to sustain their interest until the task is practiced more thoroughly during the next class session.

Summary

Practice schedules are more influential upon final levels of performance in a given learning situation than of long-term retention. Other things being equal, the manner in which an individual has acquired a task (whole versus part practice, massed versus distributed practice) is not influential of retention. Overlearning enhances retention, as does practice in tasks whose components flow together in a rhythmic, meaningful manner.

Motivation and optimum placement of rest periods are intimately related. Rest is called for when it is apparent that progress is being retarded by lack of interest or too long an exposure to the task in which improvement is desired. This rest can consist of successively longer intervals as learning is continued.

Whether an individual is exposed to a whole task or its parts is a function of the complexity of the task as well as the maturity and capabilities of the learner. Generally, it is deemed best to attempt to transmit as much of the entire task as possible at a single exposure. Whole learning is quicker and thus more motivating than laboriously and unnecessarily putting together pieces of an action pattern.

The initial portions of a series of complex task components or of a series of skills tend to obliterate and make difficult learning the middle of a series. Difficult parts of a skill, or difficult skills, should be placed near the beginning of a practice session. Skills presented during the middle portions of a practice session should be reviewed during the final parts of the session. Activities desired for emphasis should also be placed near the end of the class period, near the terminus of the school semester, or presented initially.

BIBLIOGRAPHY

1. Abbey, David S. Age proficiency and reminiscence in a complex perceptual-motor task. *Percept. and Mot. Skills,* 1962, 14, 51–57.

2. Clark, L. Verdelle. Effect of mental practice on the development of a certain motor skill. *Res. Quart.,* 1960, 31, 560–568.

3. Cratty, Bryant J. Recency vs. primacy in a complex gross motor task. *Res. Quart.,* 1963, 34, 3–8.

4. DeMonchaux, Cecily J. The effect on memory of completed and uncompleted tasks. Unpublished Ph.D. thesis, University of London Library, 1952.

5. Egstrom, Glen. The effects of an emphasis on conceptualizing techniques upon the early learning of a gross motor skill. Doctoral dissertation, University of Southern California, Los Angeles, 1961.

6. Eysenck, H. J., and Maxwell, A. E. Reminiscence as a function of drive. *Brit. J. Psychol.,* 1961, 58, 43–52.

7. Jahnke, John C. Post rest motor learning performances as a function of degree of learning. *J. Exp. Psychol.,* 1961, 62, 605–611.

8. Karlin, Lawrence, and Mortimer, Rudolph G. Effect of verbal, visual and auditory augmenting cues on learning a complex motor skill. *J. Exp. Psychol.,* 1963, 65, 75–79.

9. Koonce, Jefferson M., Chambliss, Davis J., and Irion, Arthur. Long-term reminiscence in the pursuit rotor habit. *J. Exp. Psychol.,* 1964, 67, 498–500.

10. Lavery, J. J., and Suddon, Florence H. Retention of simple motor skills as a function of the number of trials by which K of R is delayed. *Percept. and Mot. Skills,* 1962, 15, 231–237.

11. Lipman, Ronald S., and Spitz, Herman. The relationship between kinesthetic satiation and inhibition in rotary pursuit performance. *J. Exp. Psychol.,* 1961, 62, 468–475.

12. McGeogh, A. The influence of four different interpolated activities upon retention. *J. Exp. Psychol.,* 1931, 14, 400–413.

13. Naylor, James C., and Briggs, George. Effect of rehearsal of temporal and spatial aspects on the long-term retention of a procedural skill. *J. Appl. Psychol.,* 1963, 4, 120–126.

14. Pechstein, Louis A. Massed vs. distributed effort in learning. *J. Ed. Psychol.,* 1921, 12, 92–97.

15. Plutchik, Robert, and Petti, Rodger D. Rate of learning on a pursuit rotor task at a constant work rest ratio with varying work and rest ratios. *Percept. and Mot. Skills*, 1964, 19, 227–231.

16. Rubin-Rabson, Grace. Studies in the psychology of memorizing piano music: II. A comparison of massed and distributed practice. *J. Ed. Psychol.*, 1940, 31, 270–284.

17. Start, K. B. Relationship between intelligence and the effect of mental practice on the performance of a motor skill. *Res. Quart.*, 1960, 31, 644–649.

18. Twining, W. E. Mental practice and physical practice in learning a motor skill. *Res. Quart.*, 1949, 20, 432–435.

Basic assumptions about the transfer of training underlie all educational programs. In physical education classes and on athletic teams, most formal instruction is an attempt to elicit transfer in some form. Transfer is the effect that practice of one skill has upon a second.

Transfer may be negative, positive, or absent. The practice of one skill may facilitate, impede, or have no effect upon a second. A verbal description of a skill prior to practice is an attempt to elicit transfer. As a coach works on fundamentals, he is attempting to promote the transfer of simple skill components to the performance of the complex whole. The young adult often attempts to transfer his past experiences to the solution of problems currently confronting him. Learning curves are a graphic representation of the effect of one trial upon the one which follows, and illustrate a common form of transfer.

Transfer of skills may be evaluated by contrasting two separate skills performed by the same individual or group. Transfer may also be studied by noting the effect of performing and learning a skill with one hand upon the performance of the same skill with the other hand. Transfer may be studied by considering what effect practicing a skill's components has upon the whole, or studying the effect practicing the complex whole has upon performance of its parts.

A considerable amount of experimental evidence has accumulated which helps us to gain a reasonably clear picture of the variables which influence the trans-

14 Transfer of Skill

fer of training. Theories of three general types have been formulated to attempt to explain transfer. One theory postulates that the performance of one skill influences a second because of elements identical to each. A second theory suggests that two skills are mutually affective because various kinds of general elements influence the performance of both. A third, and the most acceptable theory, states that transfer of training occurs because of both general elements and specific factors influencing the performance of two or more skills.

Without a thorough knowledge of transfer, the coach or physical education teacher can impede skill learning. It is believed that the principles of transfer which follow are the most important for the educator on the athletic field to consider.

109.0 *Transfer of training may occur from limb to limb in the same individual. Practicing a task with one hand will facilitate its performance with the other* (1, 12).

One recent investigation indicated that as much skill transferred from one of the subject's hands to a second as was elicited as the subjects *watched* demonstration of the manual skill performed by another individual. Such findings indicate that skilled learning is a function of the central nervous system, not of the body-part engaged in the task.

Bilateral transfer of training is also possible from hand to foot, or vice versa. In general, the skill level of the initial limb as well as its proximity to the second limb will influence the amount of transfer occurring.

Implications. When fatigue or other learning blocks occur, practice in a complex skill such as throwing may at times be attempted with the non-dominant hand. With young children such practice is usually not considered good, particularly as they are attempting to establish a dominant hand. However, older children and adults may find this type of practice beneficial. It is frequently observed in experimental situations that performance in a difficult one-handed task is performed in a superior manner with the non-dominant hand. It has been suggested that the performer is more attentive to the movements of his non-dominant hand, and thus is more skillful when using it initially.

Complex movements of the feet while learning a game such as soccer may facilitate complex movements of the upper limbs. In all cases of this kind, the amount of bilateral transfer is greatest if the task is learned with the dominant hand and a high level of performance reached prior to attempting the same task with the opposite hand.

110.0 *Strength improvement is often apparent in a limb other than that which has been exercised* (1).

Although theoreticians a few years ago suggested that this kind of bilateral transfer of strength showed that the central nervous system was important in the development of strength, more recent evidence suggests that this transfer is caused by the individual tensing his other body parts to varying degrees when performing a forceful movement with one hand.

Implications. Expecting marked degrees of transfer of strength from one limb to a second is not realistic. Better practice is to exercise the limb one is interested in strengthening, just as learning a skill with the preferred hand is more productive.

111.0 *The most positive transfer will occur when elements of the two tasks are identical* (10).

When the responses required in the two tasks are identical or have identical components, positive transfer will occur as a person changes quickly from practice of one to performance of the second.

Implications. The coach who duplicates accurately in practice all the components of skills needed in the game will be most successful. Participating in non-specific coordination drills will not be as successful as practicing the exact components.

The writer has recently observed a water polo coach who analyzed the manner in which individuals may, within the rules, take a ball across a swimming pool. During one part of practice each day his team members are exposed to structured drills which duplicate exactly the numerous ways in which this can be accomplished, e.g., dribble, stop and look; dribble, fake, dribble; or dribble, turn, dribble.

Similarly, many successful basketball coaches engage in warm-up drills which attempt to duplicate the kinds of foot movements offensive and defensive players will be called upon to make in a game situation. Running backwards, laterally and backwards, or shuffling left and right or laterally and forward, all with the appropriate arm movements, are components of offensive and defensive play desirable for inclusion in practice drills.

112.0 *Transfer occurs from the simple to the complex as well as from the complex to the simple* (3, 7, 11).

In general, transfer from the simple components of a task will occur when they are practiced for prolonged periods of time, just as practice of the whole complex task will transfer to its simpler parts. More transfer can sometimes be expected in the latter case, although this is not always true.

Implications. At times a skill can be mastered more quickly by practicing it in its entirety and then reducing it to its parts. For example, running in American football can sometimes be practiced first as a whole and then, for purposes of refinement, be broken down into simple components, including various turns, spins, and so on. A more extensive discussion of whole versus part practice is found in Chapter 13.

113.0 *Negative transfer will occur if a response is called for in a situation which in the past required a different movement (2).*

This principle is the one most likely to be violated by both the experienced and the inexperienced coach. Experimental evidence indicates that learning a simple movement with a badminton racket, such as hitting a bird against the wall, will impede the learning of an apparently similar skill, hitting a tennis ball against a wall. In both skills similar stimulus conditions are present—a racket, an object to be hit, and a wall. However, the responses required are different. In badminton, wrist action is a primary requisite, while a relatively stiff wrist is desirable when wielding a tennis racket.

The writer has often observed centers in basketball participating in a "tip-in" drill, in which they arrange themselves on opposite sides of the basket and "tip" the ball back and forth, banking it off the backboard to each other. This drill will produce negative transfer, i.e., it will impede tipping the ball in during basketball games. Despite the fact that some hand-eye-wrist sensitivity may be developed, in essence the players are not learning to tip the ball *in* the basket, but *over* the basket. In the game, the stimulus conditions are the same, but the response called for (tipping the ball *in* the basket) is quite different from the one practiced.

Care must be taken by coaches and physical educators to practice the exact movements. To practice movements which are *nearly* the same as those of the task can be disastrous.

This principle is also violated when attempting to improve the catching skill of a young child through the use of a bean bag. It is true that it is easier to catch a bean bag than a ball, for the former literally "sticks" when it comes in contact with the hand. If the experimental evidence concerning transfer is valid, however, bean bag catching could seriously hinder the catching of balls.

While the perceptual or stimulus elements in bean bag catching and ball catching are roughly the same (an object moving toward the catcher on some relatively predictable trajectory), the response requirements of the task are different. In the former case, the hand does not have to "give" and relax when it contacts the missile; the bag can be counted on to cling to the hand. In the second case, however, the hand must relax and "give" as the ball contacts it. If this does not occur, the ball will rebound much as if it had contacted a stone wall.

114.0   *General elements sometimes transfer from task to task (2, 4, 6).*

Corollary 114.1   The ability to adopt similar work methods with success when performing several kinds of perceptual-motor tasks may facilitate learning of subsequent skills.
Corollary 114.2   "Learning how to learn" has been demonstrated to elicit positive transfer in experimental studies with children and primates.

Given a series of tasks which are roughly similar, such as various agility tasks on the football field, a certain amount of transfer will occur. Those learned last will generally be performed better than those learned initially. Individuals will not only learn the specific motions required, but will learn how to learn agility tasks. Athletes, for example, seem to learn how to pace themselves, and also how to analyze tasks of a given type upon repeated exposure to them.

Transfer due to these causes is generally not as predictable, nor does it occur to the same degree, as transfer dependent upon the training of identical movement elements. However, it does occur.

Implications.   While warm-up drills of a general nature will create a mental set in performers which may facilitate their actions during the practice period, it is usually more efficient to design practice movements, warm-up drills, and coordination drills so that their movements duplicate those of the skills in which improvement is desired.

115.0   *Transfer must be taught (4).*

The learner should always be made cognitively aware of the elements in two tasks which are identical in order for a maximum amount of positive transfer to occur.

Implications.   The coach and teacher should help the learner to analyze the motor task, and particularly to specify why he is practicing various component movements. The amount of positive transfer which will occur depends partly upon the learner's insight. Identification of identical elements can be engaged in prior to and at the completion of various practice tasks.

Helping the learner to think about identical elements will enhance the amount of transfer. He may need to be shown which components are similar. If some components are dissimilar, he should be made aware of these in order to avoid possible negative transfer. This initial differentiation of similar response elements may be carried out through verbal explanations or visual demonstrations. The extent to which this kind of "training for transfer" will be effective is based upon the ability of the learner to analyze the task with the help of the teacher.

116.0   *The higher the level of original learning achieved in the initial task, the greater the amount of transfer which will be evidenced, other things being equal (3, 9).*

Implications.   Drills effective in the training of athletes should be overlearned to be most effective. Performance should become almost reflexive in appearance for a maximum amount of transfer to occur. The greater the proficiency in the skill attained, the higher the level of final performance expected in the complex skill.

117.0   *Transfer may be impeded if a high level of performer anxiety is evident (4).*

Relaxed performers are not only better able to understand and relate common movement elements in two tasks, but are also more capable of analyzing perceptual elements common to two or more tasks.

Implications.   Practice which will hopefully be followed by transfer should be conducted in as relaxed a manner as possible. Verbal admonishments and other psychological "noises" which heighten levels of performer anxiety will tend to impede positive transfer.

118.0   *Massed practice may inhibit transfer (4).*

Drills which are prolonged and in which too much overlearning is attempted will often build resistance against performance of the type of skills in which improvement is desired. After a point, continued practice in football drills will engender a far from positive attitude toward the game.

119.0   *Skill in non-specific coordination tasks will not usually transfer to sports skills (8).*

A number of research studies have demonstrated that certain traditional coordination exercises result in improvement only in themselves. Although at times such drills may enhance subsequent performance because of the presence of some of the general elements mentioned previously, continued practice of these drills may inhibit performance by engendering a negative attitude toward similar activity.

120.0   *The greater the number of related training tasks, the more positive transfer will generally result (4).*

Implications. The coach able to devise the greatest number of drills which attempt to duplicate game conditions, while at the same time working on general strategy, can be expected to engender the greatest amount of positive transfer from practice field to the actual game. A complex task like playing halfback on an American football team requires many complex subskills (running and variations, various ways of eluding would-be tacklers, passing, and kicking). The greater the number of meaningful practice experiences to which such a performer can be subjected, the finer the performance he can be expected to exhibit in the game.

121.0   *Positive transfer can occur because of the presence of subtle "bridges" between two tasks (4).*

At times these bridges are in the form of thoughtful contemplation by the performer, and at other times in the form of lectures by the teacher and coach.

Transfer must be taught; left to chance, it is unlikely to happen to any great degree. Recently it was attempted to institute a program into schools for special education which would incorporate pattern recognition practice on the part of retardates by having them play games with triangles, rectangles, half-circles, and letter shapes on the playground. Teachers who assumed that the children would somehow connect classroom drill in pattern recognition with the playground shapes were disappointed; teachers who planned teaching programs incorporating both learning modalities (tactile-visual inspection of shapes and gross movements in the shapes) were pleased by the results obtained.

122.0   *Greatest positive transfer can be expected if effort is expended when learning the initial parts of a series of tasks (4).*

The initial parts of a series will not only prove easiest but, if they are learned well, the performer will begin to form a positive attitude about the task and his capabilities in performing it which he will tend to maintain. Earlier reference to development of a high level of aspiration is found in Chapter 3.

Summary

Physical educators are often prone to claim too quickly that transfer is taking place when in truth it is not, or cannot occur. Transfer is more to be expected when the situations and/or the specific elements in two tasks are identical. Although there is a range of similarity which encourages positive transfer, negative transfer will usually result if the differences between two tasks are moderate in nature. If the differences are obvious, neither negative nor positive transfer will be evidenced.

Transfer will not always occur by chance, but must be taught. Insight into the nature of the task as well as continued practice on a preparatory task will facilitate transfer.

From an inspection of the available literature, it is difficult to generalize as to whether transfer is more pronounced from the simple to the complex or vice versa. At the same time, it is clear that attempting to learn a new response within a familiar situation will impede transfer, particularly during the initial stages of learning the second task. Many times, during the later stages of learning, error will occur which indicates that a latent response from a previous task is interfering with performance of the present one.

Transfer is a basic phenomenon involved in attempts to improve skilled learning. Failure to understand the principles underlying this facet of performance will impede many aspects of athletic training. Knowledge of it and ability to apply the knowledge intelligently on the athletic field or in the physical education class should lead to more productive learning and performance in many athletic endeavors.

BIBLIOGRAPHY

1. Ammons, R. B. "Le Mouvement," in *Current psychological issues,* Georgene H. Seward and John P. Seward (eds.). New York: Holt, 1958.
2. Bruce, R. W. Conditions of transfer of training. *J. Exp. Psychol.,* 1933, 16, 343–361.
3. Duncan, C. P. Transfer in motor learning as a function of first task learning and inter-task similarity. *J. Exp. Psychol.,* 1953, 45, 1–11.
4. Ellis, Henry. *The transfer of learning.* New York: Macmillan, 1965.
5. Gagne, R. M., Baker, K. E., and Foster, H. *Psychology and human performance.* New York: Holt, 1959, 493.
6. Harlow, H. F. The formation of learning sets. *Psychol. Rev.,* 1949, 56, 51–65.
7. Holding, D. H. Transfer between difficult and easy tasks. *Brit. J. Psychol.,* 1962, 53, 397–407.
8. Lindeburg, Franklin A. A study of the degree of transfer between quickening exercises and other coordinated movements. *Res. Quart.,* 1949, 20, 180–195.
9. Mukherjee, Bishova Nath. Transfer of two-hand coordination skill as a function of initial ability level. *J. Gen. Psychol.,* 1962, 67, 215–223.

10. Namikas, Gediminas, and Archer, E. James. Motor skill transfer as a function of inter-task interval and pre-transfer task difficulty. *J. Exp. Psychol.*, 1960, 59, 109–112.

11. Seymour, W. Douglas. Transfer of training in engineering skills. *Percept. and Mot. Skills*, 1957, 7, 235–237.

12. Yensen, Roy. A factor influencing motor overflow. *Percept. and Mot. Skills*, 1965, 20, 967–968.

part six

GROUP INTERACTION

Mature people rarely perform without being influenced by some facet of their social environment. This influence may be exerted by the broad cultural context, which molds an individual's choice of activities and decides what levels of performance are acceptable for men and women of various ages. Sub-cultures also influence performance. The family, work group, the child's peers, and others in close proximity to the performer influence his momentary performance levels as well as the extent to which he may persist in a task.

In this chapter it is proposed to examine briefly one of the less complex kinds of relationships between performer and society, the effect of onlookers upon performance. Some social scientists have referred to an "unseen audience" composed of friends, peers, and so on, which is always present and exerts its influences even when an individual performs alone. The following pages, however, discuss the effects of audiences composed of one or more people that are physically present.

The audience and the performer may evidence various kinds of interaction. The audience may passively observe the athlete's efforts. They may subtly react to his performance negatively or positively or may, in an obvious and direct way, attempt to influence the manner in which he executes some motor skill.

All performance is usually evaluated by the individual performing by comparing himself to others of his age and experience. The presence of a reacting audi-

15 The Audience

ence gives the performer more direct and immediate evidence of the extent to which he is meeting or failing to meet society's expectations, and thus his performance can usually be depended upon to fluctuate more in the presence of onlookers. At the same time, individual performance in a group whose members are also performing is usually even more variable and susceptible to group pressure than performance in front of a group which is merely watching.

Onlookers may attempt to encourage or discourage performance in direct ways. They may also, by their very presence, influence another's efforts without any obvious attempts to do so. When one or more onlookers observe and react to the performance of another, they may subtly "catch" each other's gestures and movement patterns as a kind of "behavioral contagion" takes place (11).

An audience usually raises the tension level of the performer so that performance changes under competition; addition of some emotional stress, such as fear of failure, and similar circumstances exert roughly the same influence upon his efforts as an observer. As it was attempted within this book to include only those principles reasonably well documented by experimental evidence, this chapter is brief. There has been little substantial research dealing with audience-performer interactions, particularly those in which the performer is engaged in vigorous physical output.

Theories often advanced, however, are unsupported by any experimental evidence. For example, it is sometimes assumed that, with continued exposure to the stress of an audience, an individual learns to accommodate reactions produced by onlookers, and performance decrements due to excess tension become less. However, the writer is unaware of research which supports this contention.

Coaches frequently refer to the advantage of a home team when performing in front of an audience sympathetic to its efforts. However, research previously cited in Chapter 4 suggests that young children may perform better in front of a *disliked* peer than when only a friend is present (14). Thus the advantage of playing on "friendly ground" may lie in familiarity with the dimensions of the court or the benevolence of "home" officiating rather than the presence of a congenial audience.

Recent surveys involving thorough analyses of the feelings of university-college and professional athletes about their fans have strongly suggested that athletes not only dislike their supporters, but frequently evidence deep-seated hostility toward them. Although much of the time these feelings seem repressed, this evidence is understandable from two standpoints.

1. Athletes are well aware of the manner in which the allegiance of their more rabid fans fluctuates. The athlete is lauded when he wins and

reaps ridicule when he fails. It is not difficult to understand reservations the athlete must have concerning the accolades of his spectators, particularly those who currently seem to support him to the fullest.

2. Athletes usually feel that spectators are somehow seeking status through their efforts. The artist often has some disdain for those buying his art for the same reason. To enhance the feelings of others through strenuous and taxing physical effort cannot help but engender a certain amount of resentment toward those who simply "ride on their backs."

The interaction of maturation and the "audience-effect" has been previously reviewed in Chapter 5. Generally, the presence of an onlooker observing the performance of a child younger than six will have little or no measurable effect upon his performance. If the onlooker is a friend, there will at times be a decrement in performance because of the distractability of a youngster of this age. Although children below the age of six will evidence some general excitability when placed in front of an audience, this heightened level of arousal does not usually translate itself into performance improvement (as is often the case with youngsters older than six).

One respected European researcher has suggested that a real awareness of the social implications of good performance is not grasped until after a child reaches the age of six. Prior to that time, the child has no sound concept of how he can direct the heightened levels of tension he experiences into concrete performance improvement (9).

It is often difficult to separate the effects of an audience from performance changes elicited as individuals interact directly with one another. For example, as two men execute a block together, their effort is probably enhanced both because they are striking another player simultaneously and because they are aware of and are reacting to a teammate's very presence.

At the same time, individuals performing in close proximity or merely placed in one another's presence frequently interfere with each other's performance in various ways. Stress is catching. The coach who becomes excitable on the bench frequently transmits his feelings, with a resultant loss in efficiency, to the members of the team. The negative and positive effects of group interaction and simple group facilitation (the audience effect) are at times indivisible.

The findings which follow, however, deal with situations in which there are one or more onlookers and a single performer. More complex group interactions are discussed in the chapters which follow. Furthermore, the onlookers are assumed not to be engaged in performance themselves, but are influencing the performer to varying degrees by their presence and/or by some kind of discouraging or encouraging verbal behavior.

123.0   *The presence of an audience raises the tension level of the performer (2, 4, 10).*

The effects of an audience upon performance may be expected to be similar to those observed when muscular tension is raised.

Corollary 123.1   Performance in endurance tasks is usually improved in the presence of onlookers (13).

Research indicates that bicycle riding and various experimental tasks, including treadmill running and finger flexion endurance, are improved in the presence of one or more persons.

Corollary 123.2   An audience has been demonstrated to improve performance in simple strength tasks in which direct forceful action is called for.

Corollary 123.3   When performing more complex perceptual-motor tasks, the presence of an audience has been demonstrated to enhance the performance of some while impeding the performance of others.

Whether performance is facilitated or inhibited seems to depend upon whether the individual is already working up to the optimum level of tension called for by the particular task. Poor performers in simple tasks are aided when placed in front of an audience, whereas good performers in the same task are sometimes impeded because they are already working within optimum tension limits. More complex performance can usually be depended upon to become more variable when individuals in a group are confronted with an audience.

124.0   *The extent to which an individual evidences performance change when confronted with an audience seems to depend upon his familiarity with the task.*

Accommodation to the pressure of onlookers, while perhaps at times a general attribute, seems largely dependent upon the individual's self assurance gained from past experience in a specific task. For example, a recent research study indicated that when the performances of a *laboratory task* of athletes and non-athletes were compared before and after the introduction of onlookers, no significant differences were evidenced.

Findings of this nature indicate that athletes may learn to relax in front of an audience only while performing a specific set of skills (a sport). A football player playing basketball in front of an audience would be expected to evidence the same disruption of performance as a novice playing basketball in front of onlookers. On the other hand, a basketball player, after frequent exposures to the pressure of others watching, may be expected to accommodate his basketball performance to the resultant pressures.

Implications. The coach can often elicit performance changes by suggesting to the performer that various individuals will "hold him to account" for his later efforts, i.e., in essence, by attempting to construct an unseen audience. Care must be taken, however, not to raise tension levels in this manner to the detriment of performance.

Teams and individuals seem able to be taught to accommodate the presence of an audience. Athletes acquire poise after repeated confrontations with friendly and hostile audiences. The sparse experimental literature on this question suggests that this accommodation is specific to the task. Basketball players can play a good game of basketball after several seasons of audience pressure. Suddenly converting these same athletes to another, less familiar, sport, and placing them in a position in which they will be seen by others, can probably be counted upon to elicit confusion and result in a disruption of their performance in the second sport.

Calling athletes' attention to the feelings of the fickle home crowd or the hostile visiting crowd may sometimes produce desirable tension changes. As has been suggested, few good athletes have positive feelings about those who seem to be attempting to gain status from their "sweat." At times these hostile feelings may be exploited.

> **125.0**   *The effect of an audience upon performance is partly dependent upon the previous relationship between the onlooker(s) and the performer.*

Corollary 125.1   Individuals who have had a close social relationship with the performer can be counted upon to severely impede the accurate performance of perceptual-motor skills (6, 7).

One research study supporting this corollary found that "razzing" by an individual's fraternity brothers elicited considerable stress, which was reflected in performance decrements.

Corollary 125.2   Admonishment by individuals not well known to the performer can be expected to have relatively little effect upon his performance (12).

In general, the closer two individuals are socially, the more effect praise or heckling by one will have upon the performance of the other.

Implications. The coach should probably be more sensitive to interpersonal blame or praise within the team than to praise or blame coming from spectators. Team members who constantly "ride" other members begin to lose their status, and the effect of their negativisms probably becomes less. On the other hand, a coach can frequently change the performance of a member of the team drastically by having one of the more respected members of the team talk to him. Many times the team leader can exert a more profound influence upon the performance of a boy than anyone else.

126.0   *Persistence in a task is a general quality which is more marked when some kind of social stimulation is introduced (15).*

Willingness to endure discomfort in both motor and mental tasks in the presence of social approval has been found to be a general quality.

127.0   *Some individuals, usually the better athletes, have high needs for social approval.*

This personality trait has been shown to evidence moderate and positive correlations with the ability to perform reasonably complex gross motor skills.

Although some individuals, usually the more mature, seem to participate in vigorous athletics simply because they enjoy experiencing some kind of self-improvement, most of those who excel in athletics have a relatively high need for social recognition which they attempt to satisfy by successful participation in sports.

The so-called spectator sports are usually entered into by individuals who not only possess helpful physical qualities, but are acutely aware of the social rewards for athletic success and covet the status they can achieve. This kind of feeling is frequently exploited by the coach in his attempts to extract superior performance by appealing to the social approval and punishments inherent in the situation—"The team is counting on you, and so is the whole student body!"

Implications.   Social approval is an obvious reward for athletic success, particularly in sports recognized by the culture or sub-culture as "important." An overdependence on this kind of external motivator can, however, exert a detrimental effect when the youth leaves school. If his participation in vigorous activity has been primarily to achieve status rather than for the game's intrinsic values, he will frequently discontinue his pursuit of the sport in later years and lose the concomitant physiological and psychological advantages of participation for its own sake.

Individual sports athletes who have practiced "carry-over" sports, in which relatively little social approval is sometimes involved, have formed a better psychological basis for continued participation when social approval is absent. Their previous participation has often been for the sake of the sport rather than for the status rewards to be gained.

It would seem important to encourage athletes in "high status" sports to gain proficiencies in recreational activities other than their major sports.

If the major sport can be participated in after school days are over, the athlete should be encouraged to do so. If continued participation in the sport will be difficult without the presence of teammates or crowds, the coach and physical educator seem obligated to attempt to broaden the athlete's interests, and introduce him to various recreational activities which he may pursue in later years.

Summary

The onlooker raises the tension level of the performer so that ability changes evidenced are a function of the amount of tension already present as well as the tension requirements of the task. Simple forceful movements are usually facilitated by the presence of an audience, as is the performance of endurance tasks.

Performance in complex skills may be improved or impeded when others are watching, depending upon the familiarity of the performer with the task as well as the extent to which he has practiced it in the presence of concomitant social pressure.

Onlookers change the behavior of the performer by their very presence, through their actions, and by the degree of approval or disapproval they voice. Spectators can be expected to have a more marked influence upon a performer if they have enjoyed a previously close social contact. On the other hand, superior athletes have been demonstrated to possess an underlying disdain for the noisy and fickle spectator.

BIBLIOGRAPHY

1. Abel, Theodora M. The influence of social facilitation on motor performance at different levels of intelligence. *Amer. J. Psychol.*, 1938, 51, 379–389.

2. Cox, F. N. Some effects of test anxiety and presence or absence of other persons on boys' performance on a repetitive motor task. *J. of Exp. Child Psychol.*, 1965, 3, 100–112.

3. Dashiell, J. F. Experimental studies of the influence of social situations on the behavior of individual human adults, in *Handbook of social psychology*. Worchester, Mass.: Clark Univ. Press, 1935.

4. Gates, G. S., and Rissland, L. Q. The effect of encouragement and of discouragement upon performance. *J. Ed. Psychol.*, 1923, 14, 21–26.

5. Hollingworth, H. L. *The psychology of the audience.* New York: American Book Company, 1935.

6. Icheiser, G. Changes in performance through consciousness of a spectator. *Zsch. Psychotechn.*, 1930, 5, 52–53.

7. Laird, D. A. Changes in motor control and individual variations under the influence of "razzing." *J. Exp. Psychol.*, 1923, 6, 236–246.

8. Lewis, Michael, Wall, Martin, and Aronfreed, Justin. Developmental change in the relative values of social and non-social reinforcement. *J. of Exp. Psychol.*, 1963, 66, 133–137.

9. Missiuro, W. The development of reflex activity in children, in *International research in sport and physical education*, E. Jokl (ed.). Springfield, Illinois: Charles C. Thomas, 1964, 372–383.

10. Pessin, J., and Husband, R. W. Effects of social stimulants on human maze learning. *J. Abn. Soc. Psychol.*, 1933, 28, 148–154.

11. Redl, F. Group emotion and leadership. *Psychiatry*, 1942, 5, 573–596.

12. Stevenson, H. W. Social reinforcement with children as a function of CA., sex of E. and sex of S. *J. Abn. Soc. Psychol.*, 1961, 63, 147–154.

13. Triplett, N. The dynamogenic factors in pace-making and competition. *Amer. J. Psychol.*, 1898, 9, 507–533.

14. Wardweel, Elinor. Childrens' reactions to being watched during success and failure. Unpublished Doctoral dissertation, Cornell University, 1960.

15. Willington, Ama M., and Strickland, Bonnie R. Need for approval and simple motor performance. *Percept. and Mot. Skills*, 1964, 21, 879–884.

Individuals form groups for a variety of reasons. At times, the need for mutual affiliation for "good fellowship" is the primary motive. At other times, solution of some kind of problem, e.g., winning football games, provides the impetus. Groups formed because the members value each other's companionship are sometimes called primary groups by the social psychologists, while those formed for a more specific purpose are termed secondary groups.

As group members interact with each other and work as a group against or with others, they tend to evidence varying degrees of cohesiveness. If placed under a moderate amount of stress, group members become closer to one another, just as they do when they experience success while mutually interacting.

Various factors bring people together and cause formation of friendships. Similarity in interests and values, as well as simply being in close proximity for a prolonged time, have been found to influence the appearance of friendships. Two or more people may also tend to "pull apart" from one another after working together for a period of time in solution of some kind of task.

Teamwork is one of the most used and least understood words in the vocabulary of the coach and physical educator. It will be the purpose of this chapter to attempt to add depth to the meaning of this important term. The statements are based upon evidence gained from the literature in social psychology, research which

16 Group Affiliation and Cohesion

has involved athletic participation, and observation of performing and learning motor skills in the laboratory. Principles which relate specifically to cooperation and competition between individuals and groups are found in Chapter 18.

128.0 *There is a group factor, operative in performance tasks involving integration of the efforts of at least two people, which is relatively independent of individual ability (2).*

Corollary 128.1   The ability to integrate one's movements with another's and to anticipate the actions of one's partner is somewhat independent of the ability to perform alone (2).

Implications.   It is frequently found by coaches in team sports, doubles tennis, and similar activities that players who perform best individually do not help the group effort when placed with similar "stars."

While there is, of course, a moderate relationship between individual and group ability in high level performance, the coach making up a team would do well to search for individuals on his roster who perform best in groups, rather than being too influenced by individual efforts. This group attribute involves the ability to anticipate the movements of another individual (e.g., to pass well to a breaking man in basketball or to the end in football); this response is relatively independent of the ability to handle a ball and throw it in situations extraneous to the game.

This quality probably involves a type of perceptual anticipation important when tracking balls in flight. For the coach to simply place individual "stars" on a team and hope for the best group effort is to court disaster. He should search for individuals who work well together, know their teammates' unique characteristics, and accommodate well to each other's unique action patterns.

129.0 *Individuals will form friendships if they are in relatively close physical proximity to one another (8, 11).*

Corollary 129.1   Friendship patterns in summer camps have been experimentally altered by breaking up and reforming athletic teams (9).

When friends were separated in this manner, they tended to affiliate less; different friendships were established on the newly formed teams.

Corollary 129.2   Friendships in housing developments and in offices have been found to be predictable primarily by noting the location of adjacent apartments and desks (5, 8).

Implications.   Close association on athletic teams, independent of winning or losing, will tend to facilitate the formation of friendships. The coach should be sensitive to the role he plays in structuring the social strata of the school in which he is working. Instructors of athletic teams may, at times, promote greater understanding between two boys by placing them on the same team. Other things being equal, the placement of boys in this manner will hopefully aid mutual acceptance and respect.

130.0 *Friendships will be more likely to form between individuals who are similar in abilities, attitudes, and interests (6, 11).*

Corollary 130.1 Conversely, friends will tend to view each other as similar even though the similarities may not be as marked as they both assume.

Implications. Cliques in schools and on athletic teams will more likely be formed by individuals of similar ability. Those of similar athletic ability will tend to view each other as similar in such other ways as intellect, attitude, and values, and may thus instill values and attributes in one another. This influence of friends upon one another will at times be detrimental to their character and at times be an asset. The coach should be particularly sensitive to the strong influence better members of the team may exert upon the school community and upon individuals of lesser ability. If the direction of this influence seems ill advised, individual counseling may be called for.

131.0 *When working together toward a goal (or goals), success achieved by an individual is usually at least partly attributed to the presence and abilities of other members of the group (14).*

Corollary 131.1 When individual success is achieved in a group situation, some of the good feelings about success will transfer even to an observer (14).
Corollary 131.2 When repeated failure is encountered in a group situation, at least part of the failure is usually attributed by an individual to other members of the group (11).

The relative success, or lack of it, experienced in group activities, e.g., games, is always attributed, in some measure, by individuals in the group to the behavior of other members. Success breeds greater mutual cohesion, while failure, if encountered for a prolonged period, should tend to make the group less cohesive.

Implications. The coach and physical education instructor should be aware of the tendency of individuals to transfer their feelings of frustration over failure to other members of the team. This transference, or scapegoating, can at times so impede collective performance as to render group effectiveness inoperative. Individuals on teams should be aided in gaining the maturity to assume their share of the blame following loss as well as the credit for winning a game. This kind of character training should serve most youth in good stead later in life.

132.0   *Stress applied to a group may aid group cohesion (9).*

Stress in the form of losing games may at first weld a team closer together and result in the group resolution that they will "try harder."

Corollary 132.1   Continued stress over a period of time will tend to heighten mutual dissatisfaction among group members, and break down group cohesion (9).

Repeated failure, either to win or to work up to the potential of the group, will result in lowering of morale to the point where, if given the choice, the group will disintegrate. Individual members may then seek others with whom they achieve some kind of success.

133.0   *The need to affiliate and the need to achieve are both satisfied in athletic participation.*

Corollary 133.1   Individuals who have a high need for achievement will tend to pick a teammate or work partner who performs well, regardless of the degree of friendship involved (5).

Corollary 133.2   Individuals who have a high need for affiliation will tend to pick a teammate or work partner who is their friend, regardless of his ability (8).

Corollary 133.3   A specific group may tend to consist mainly of individuals together primarily for affiliative needs or associated primarily to perform well on a given task (3, 4).

It is thus suggested that there is an optimum amount of "affiliative need" and an optimum amount of "performance need" within a group to elicit the best group effort. It has been frequently observed in experimental tasks and in life that too much "social noise" can interfere with effective group interaction.

Corollary 133.4   One investigation has demonstrated that the more successful basketball teams evidence a moderate amount of inter-member hostility, particularly between the better and poorer performers (5).

Corollary 133.5   Captains, i.e., leaders, of a sports team are not always those most liked, but usually they are the more proficient players.

Implications.   Essentially, there seems to be an optimum amount of cohesion and social interaction which results in the best group effort.

Teams performing best, however, will be primarily oriented toward good performance rather than toward the need to affiliate with each other.

Consideration of the previous statements makes it clear that the degree to which a team wins or loses will affect group cohesion and orientation toward the task, and thus affect future performance.

For example, if a team is moderately successful it is to be expected that a marked amount of mutual attraction will develop among members. With more prolonged association and continued winning, they will interact further and will, many times, begin to incorporate each other into their social lives. As this happens, problems may arise relative to a continued orientation toward the initial group goal, e.g., winning football games. With further social interaction, sociality in itself may begin to subordinate the reason they initially began to interact, thus impairing group efforts on the field while facilitating mutual ability to give good weekend parties.

Conversely, a team that loses occasionally is likely to become closely knit. Moderate external group stress is usually found to bring the members closer together. Here again an optimum may be reached. With continued lack of success, the members will tend to blame one another and "pull apart," thus impeding further group efforts and establishing a relatively irrevocable failure-stress group disintegration cycle.

It would thus seem that the most successful teams are those in which winning does not begin to reorient the original focus upon good performance. A successful group should realize that continued success should involve subordination, to some extent, of individual needs to form close social affiliations among members.

It is not meant that group members must be hostile toward one another in order to achieve; on the contrary, there must be a moderate amount of "we" feeling among group members for the group to function in the first place. However, when members of a team perceive the team and its success syndrome primarily as a place in which their social needs will be met, team performance will suffer.

It is the obligation of the coach to be sensitive to these shifts in group feelings, and to anticipate the point at which social interactions may begin to subordinate the group's desire to win and achieve. The frequent practice of placing team members in adjacent living quarters on the college campus is questionable upon review of the above statements. The group members should be made to realize that their good feelings about an athletic team stem from the fact that they are *achieving* together, rather than simply because they are together. Proximity to one another, plus the fact that they are placed under varying degrees of stress and pressure, will cement friendships. However, if establishment of friendships becomes an end in itself, group efficiency may suffer.

134.0   *The group size affects the feelings its members have about their participation (11, 12).*

Corollary 134.1   With increased size, each member's involvement in the performance of a group task diminishes (12).

Corollary 134.2   As the size increases, the actual contribution of each member as well as the percentage each additional member contributes to the performance of a task diminishes. There is a loss of efficiency with the addition of members to a group (12).

Corollary 134.3   Larger groups, other things being equal, perform a task better than smaller groups because more physical and mental resources are brought to bear upon the problems (12).

Implications.   There tends to be a closer identification with the group by each individual member when it is smaller than when it is larger. In smaller groups, the contribution of an individual to the group effort is instantly apparent; members of small groups are more likely to perform well and to expend optimum efforts.

There may be an optimum size desirable for various athletic teams. While it is commonly held as sound educational policy for the coach to keep on a team as many boys as can endure the workout, it may be unsound to maintain a roster with too many names on it.

The statement above also suggests that such smaller teams as basketball and tennis will tend to evidence more group cohesion than athletic units which are larger, such as the football team. If this is the case, implications for the coach of the latter sport are obvious. It is usually found, for example, that there is less feeling of loyalty to the group among members of larger units. Therefore, the coach and physical education instructor may have to plan specific techniques in order to encourage higher group cohesion among members of larger teams.

Summary

The literature leaves no doubt that performance in groups is superior in nearly all cases to performance in isolation. Group members mutually stimulate each other by their very presence, and inform each other of the best methods to be utilized. The group holds more past experiences than can be gathered by a single individual working in isolation.

The length of time a group has been together, its size, as well as its relative success and failure, all influence the amount of group cohesion. There seems to be an optimum amount of group cohesion desirable in winning teams. Those teams whose members place affiliative needs above their needs for performance excellence will be less successful than teams whose members reverse these two goals.

Whenever people affiliate to perform a group task, varying amounts of competition and cooperative behavior are evidenced. Chapter 18 further explores these interactions by focusing upon competition and cooperation between and within groups.

Chapter 17 deals with another common element in group interactions—leadership. Whenever individuals confront each other, even if performance in some task is not apparently called for, they will attempt to arrange some hierarchy of power. Leadership to varying degrees is found in every group of two, three, or more people. At the same time, leadership is a word frequently used in various ways in connection with athletic endeavors. The material which follows presents statements which relate to the leadership of groups engaged in sports performance.

BIBLIOGRAPHY

1. Church, Russell M. The effects of competition on reaction time and palmar skin conductance. *J. Abn. Soc. Psychol.*, 1962, 65, 32–40.
2. Comrey, Andrew L., and Deskin, G. Further results on group manual dexterity in men. *J. Appl. Psychol.*, 1954, 38, 116.
3. Cooley, Charles H. *Social organization*. New York: Scribner's, 1909.
4. Cratty, Bryant J., and Sage, Jack N. The effects of primary and secondary group interaction upon improvement in a complex movement task. *Res. Quart.*, 1965, 35, 265–274.
5. Fiedler, F. E., Washington, W. G., and Blaisdell, F. G. Unconscious attitudes as correlates of sociometric choice in a social group. *J. Abn. Soc. Psychol.*, 1952, 47, 790–796.
6. French, Robert L. Sociometric status and individual adjustment among naval recruits. *J. Abn. Soc. Psychol.*, 1951, 46, 64–72.
7. Jones, Stephen, and Vroom, Victor H. Division of labor and performance under cooperative and competition conditions. *J. Abn. Soc. Psychol.*, 1964, 68, 313–320.
8. Lott, A. J., and Lott, Bernice E. Influence of classroom group cohesiveness on learning and adherence to standards. Kentucky Research Foundation, University of Kentucky, Lexington, Kentucky, 1964.
9. Pepitone, A., and Kleiner, R. The effects of threat and frustration on group cohesiveness. *J. Abn. Soc. Psychol.*, 1957, 54, 192–199.
10. Shaw, M. E. Some motivational factors in cooperation and competition. *J. Pers.*, 1959, 27, 155–169.
11. Sherif, M., and Sherif, Carolyn. *Groups in harmony and tension*. New York: Harper, 1953.

12. Thomas, E. J., and Fink, C. F. Effects of group size. *Psychol. Bull.*, 1963, 60, 371–384.

13. Wiest, W. M., Porter, L. W., and Gheselli, E. E. Individual proficiency and team performance. *J. Appl. Psychol.*, 1961, 45, 435–440.

14. Wilson, Warner, and Miller, Norman. Shifts in evaluations of participants following inter-group competition. *J. Abn. Psychol.*, 1961, 63, 428–431.

Frequent references are made by participants and coaches to various relationships between leadership and physical activity. Selection of the team captain is always an important part of any athletic season. Some authorities have suggested that athletic participation enhances an individual's potential for leadership, while there is no question that skill in physical activities contributes positively to an adolescent boy's place in the status hierarchy.

Leadership in athletic contests is usually apparent in some form. The coach searches for a "take charge" man on the basketball floor and football field. Being selected team captain is considered a unique honor. Any time individuals are in groups for the purpose of solving problems as obvious as the winning of games, some kind of leadership will emerge. Indeed, there are usually struggles for power even in discussion groups which have no such definite aims.

Writings by zoologists attest to the basic nature of status seeking. One of the classic studies in leadership involves analysis of the "pecking order" in a hen house. The herpatologists report that a hierarchy of leadership has been viewed in animals as unsophisticated as the garden lizard.

A search of the literature relating principles of leadership directly to situations in which vigorous group activity is taking place reveals more folklore than fact. For example, there is relatively little evidence that participation in athletics changes the per-

17 Leadership

sonalities of youth involved. There is no clear delineation between principles of leadership operative in team-sport situations and principles explaining the phenomena of leadership in other contexts.

The clear-cut manner in which participation in sports skills decides a winner and a loser and assesses the relative abilities of people provides an interesting laboratory in which leadership has been studied with various degrees of objectivity. It is from these kinds of investigations that the following statements were gleaned.

> **135.0** *Leadership can be assumed in a variety of ways (3, 6, 9, 10).*

Corollary 135.1 Leaders can be appointed by a higher authority.

Corollary 135.2 Leaders can be selected by the group, usually because of their prowess.

Corollary 135.3 Leadership can be seized by a group member.

A leader has been defined as the individual perceived by the group as best able to solve the group's problem(s). It is apparent, however, that most athletic teams contain several kinds of leaders at various levels. The coach is a type of leader appointed by higher authority. One or more members of the team are either vying for a leadership role or have assumed leadership because of some tacit edict from the group members or some personal need for status.

Implications. There seems no question that the best leaders are those perceived by the group as best able to enhance the group endeavor(s). The sensitive coach or physical education instructor should be aware of the team member upon whom the group is bestowing the mantle of leadership. At times, it is appropriate to work through such a boy when attempting to reach individual team members about personal problems and/or their athletic performance.

At the same time, the coach should realize that, because of the benevolence of the board of education and the principal, he has been made a type of leader over the group. In addition to acquiring leadership because of legal structure, it is hoped that, in other ways, the coach and physical education instructor will earn a portion of the leadership bestowed by the group. Pursuit of excellence by obtaining up-to-date information for the team, as well as providing an exemplary behavior model for those in his charge, are two obvious ways in which the appointed leader may enhance his position by obtaining status from the group itself.

> **136.0** *The appointed leader or emergent leader can exert varying degrees of authority upon his subordinates (7, 11).*

The leader can assume most or all of the responsibility for making decisions, or can leave some or all of the decision-making to the group members.

There is no dearth of literature dealing with the effects of authoritarianism exerted in group situations. Studies of this nature are common in texts dealing with group interactions in the business world, and with the solution of problems in military or educational settings. It is generally held that extreme authoritarianism breeds intra-group hostility. On the other hand, a certain amount of control may be necessary for purposes of efficiency and, at times, safety. Larger groups usually tolerate a greater degree of strict control by their leaders than smaller groups.

Implications. The amount of directive leadership the appointed leader (coach or physical education teacher) may effectively exert is dependent upon several variables. The quality and quantity of his past association with the group, the competencies of the group, and the nature of the task(s) facing the group are only some of the factors affecting the extent to which leadership and decision-making might be delegated to the team members.

Sound educational practice usually holds that the teacher should first present a structure and then, as group members seem able to formulate their own effective structure, remove some of the rules and decision-making in which he formerly engaged. If such procedures are followed vigorously, participation will be evidenced by team-class members, and fewer inter-group hostilities will usually be seen. It will usually be observed that students permitted to make some of the decisions regarding evaluation, activities, and so on, will subsequently think more about what they are doing rather than merely responding to whistles and commands.

There are situations on the athletic field and in the swimming pool in which the extreme stress of all-out performance must be practiced in order to effect physiological change. This kind of training usually requires that individual participants endure, to varying degrees, discomfort caused by oxygen debt and/or all-out muscular exertion. It is doubtful that most participants on track teams, for example, will voluntarily choose to punish themselves as much as seems necessary to elicit continual improvement in distance running. It has been apparent to the writer, however, that even within these situations, more vigorous performance can be elicited if team members are given an intellectual understanding of the physiological principles involved, i.e., are told *why* they hurt and the necessity for maximum effort. Even the most authoritarian swimming, track, or football coach can only exert *external* pressure upon participants. If they are viewed as humans capable of understanding *why* they must feel discomfort, they should begin to exert personal pressure to succeed which will accompany external exhortations from the coach. Additional comments relative to the need for the superior athlete to seek rather than avoid pain are found in Chapter 19.

Leadership control may thus be placed on a continuum from leader-centered to group-centered. The place on the continuum at which the appointed leader may choose to operate depends upon his analysis of the situation, appraisal of himself, including his personal needs for status and authority, and correct interpretation of the capabilities and needs of those in his charge. The point on such a continuum may shift from time to time, depending upon experiences the leader and followers have together, their relative success at the sport at hand, and the success and failures experienced as a result of the manner in which decision-making has been divided between them. With continued successful interaction, the coach can usually begin to pass some authority to members of the team. This transfer of authority is usually indicative of a desirable education program, as opposed to a mere training situation in which small muscles are made larger.

> **137.0**   *Leaders usually evidence identifiable traits. At times these traits are assumed because an individual feels he has been selected as a leader (7).*

Corollary 137.1   Leaders of sports teams are usually a little larger, a little more capable in athletics, and a little more intelligent than the other team members. If intellectual differences between team member and leader are too great, however, the leader's efforts may be impeded (3).

Corollary 137.2   Group leaders are those more sensitive to the preference hierarchy within the group (7).

Leaders are more sensitive to the friendships in the group and the needs of various group members relative to affiliation and performance.

Leaders in sports situations are thus likely to be endowed physically and with certain insights relative to group interaction. Leaders, i.e., captains, of sports teams are at times not the best liked, but rather those whom the group members perceive as best able to meet successfully the tasks facing the group.

Implications. It is fairly well substantiated that leadership, within limits, is trainable. The sensitive coach or physical educator, upon considering the above statements and their corollaries (particularly Corollary 137.2), may aid a boy to become a more effective leader by introducing him to these principles and helping him become more sensitive to the interactions of the group he is to lead. Frequently, coaches simply look for superior performers when selecting a captain, rather than for boys who are sensitive to each other and to the needs and friendships of the group members. It would seem that both physical ability and a kind of "behavioral sensitivity" are necessary for a boy to become a successful leader of a sports team. Respect, rather than simply friendship, seems to play an important role as an athletic team confers leadership on one of its members.

The effective coach and physical educator should engage in deliberate attempts to enhance the leadership potential of boys assigned to that role. Information concerning effective leadership behavior, group communication, forces and preference hierarchy within the group, and similar teachings should aid a boy to fulfill his role as a leader.

> **138.0** The individual who emerges from a group as its leader is determined partly by the characteristics of the situation (1, 2, 4).

Corollary 138.1   Leaders in social situations cannot be counted upon to be selected by the same group when confronted with tasks involving physical skill (1, 2, 4).

Corollary 138.2   Individuals who attempt to retain the leadership of a group they have acquired for tasks unlike those immediately facing the group are likely to become ineffective (4).

Corollary 138.3   Leadership effectiveness is enhanced when the group is relatively cohesive, as little "leadership energy" is expended to keep the group together and may be directed toward solution of the task(s) at hand (7).

Upon consideration of statements 137.0 and 138.0, it is apparent that leadership is a product of both the situation and the traits of individuals available in a given situation. This should be kept in mind when selecting team captains and otherwise attempting to enhance leadership potential of individuals on athletic teams.

The teacher or coach should not expect that a member of the group can function at his optimum as leader if the group members are somewhat at odds with one another. The coach may have to first attempt to manipulate the situation to enhance group cohesion before delegating some of his leadership responsibilities to a team member.

There will be a tendency among many adolescents to establish leaders in a social situation and, when transferring tasks to the athletic field, attempt to keep the same leader. At times, the individual leader involved will so covet his status in the first situation that he will go to great lengths to maintain his superiority in the second. The most effective leaders, however, have consistently been demonstrated to be those selected by the group for knowledge about and performance in the *specific situation* confronting the group. Although there are certain personality traits which seem to contribute to general leadership quality, such as the willingness to act, in most cases leadership is specific to the task.

139.0   *The physical placement of two or more individuals will enhance the chances of some for a leadership role (5).*

Corollary 139.1   The placement of chairs in which group members sit will tend to confer leadership on some, while giving others less chance for evidencing and experiencing leadership.

Corollary 139.2   It has been found that members of the baseball infield are more likely to assume managerial roles after their playing days are over (5).

It has been suggested that this tendency is due to previous opportunities to interact frequently with other team members, unlike the isolated players in the outfield.

Certain positions on various sports teams can bestow potentially greater amounts of leadership upon members occupying them than do other positions. The catcher in baseball is traditionally a team leader, as are the goalies in soccer and waterpolo, because of their opportunities to view the play and their ability to direct the energies of other members from where they stand (swim).

Implications.   There are two important implications for the coach arising from the above statements. He should be sure that certain leadership positions are occupied by individuals with high potential for assuming responsibility, based upon assessment of their ability and personality traits. Certain people who are reluctant to assume leadership roles may be encouraged to do so by placing them in "key" positions on the team.

140.0   *Successful participation in athletics by males from the ages of 6 to 20 will tend to enhance their status and potential for leadership (8).*

Corollary 140.1   Status is conferred depending upon the degree of excellence exhibited (8).

Corollary 140.2   Mere athletic participation on teams or individual sports has not been demonstrated to exert marked changes in the personality dynamics of the less skilled boy, nor does it seem to enhance his acceptability by the group for a leadership role.

Status and leadership are conferred for superior performance in athletics, not for simply being there! To manufacture competitive situations for middle and late adolescents in an effort to change their personality structure and make them better leaders is usually ineffectual. By middle and late adolescence a boy knows rather exactly his athletic potential, the degree to which he is likely to lose or win in innumerable competitive situations, and the extent to which he may be expected to elicit group approval or ridicule for his efforts in a variety of skills.

Self-improvement is a more important motivator than competition for individuals between 14 and 18 years of age. Subjecting an inept boy to competitive situations without first attempting to improve his skill may make him withdraw further, rather than "bringing him out of himself," as is sometimes intended.

The inclination of the male adolescent to participate vigorously in athletics is a function of certain personality traits, including the need for achievement and social approval as well as status, coupled with inherent and acquired physical attributes. To utilize competitive athletics as a tool to enhance the leadership potential of certain individuals, as is practiced in several of the service academies, seems naive.

Summary

Leaders will invariably emerge in competitive athletics and in games in physical education classes. These leaders are sometimes selected by a higher authority, or may seize leadership, or be given group approval for a leadership role.

Leadership is relatively specific to the task. Individuals best able to direct group efforts toward a mutually satisfying conclusion in one situation may not be so prepared in another situation involving a different kind of task.

Status is acquired for successful participation in athletic skills relative to the abilities of the other group members. Using competitive athletics as a tool with which to fashion leaders does not seem realistic.

The degree of authoritarianism evidenced by a leader may be marked or slight. Successful completion of a task is usually dependent upon how well the leader is able to assess himself, the situation, and his subordinates prior to selecting an appropriate degree of authority to exert. Generally, the effective educator should initially present his own structure and gradually, as team members or class members seem capable, transfer more and more decision-making to them.

Leadership is a function of the situation, the kind of task facing the group, as well as of the attributes of those available to lead. Knowledge of and ability to apply the above principles should prove an asset to the physical educator and to the coach.

BIBLIOGRAPHY

1. Carter, Launor F., Haythorn, William, Shriver, Beatrice, and Lanzella, John. The behavior of leaders and other group members. *J. Abn. Soc. Psychol.*, 1951, 46, 589–595.

2. ———, Haythorne, W., and Howell, M. A further investigation of the criteria of leadership. *J. Abn. Soc. Psychol.*, 1950, 45, 350–358.

3. Cratty, Bryant J. *Social dimensions of physical activity*, Chap. V, Leadership, status and physical activity. Englewood Cliffs, N.J.: Prentice-Hall, 1967.

4. ———, and Sage, Jack N. The effects of primary and secondary group interaction upon improvement in a complex movement task. *Res. Quart.*, 1964, 35, 265–274.

5. Grusky, Oscar. The effects of formal structure on managerial recruitment: a study of baseball organization. *Sociometry*, 1963, 26, No. 3, 143–146.

6. Hardy, Martha C. Social recognition at the elementary school age. *J. Soc. Psychol.*, 1937, 8, 365–386.

7. Jenkins, W. D. A review of leadership studies with particular reference to military problems. *Psychol. Bull.*, 1947, 44, 54–79.

8. Jones, Mary C. Psychological correlates of somatic development. *Child Dev.*, 1965, 33, 899–911.

9. Lott, A. J., and Lott, Bernice E. Influence of classroom group cohesiveness on learning and adherence to standards. Kentucky Research Foundation, University of Kentucky, Lexington, Kentucky, 1964.

10. Parten, Mildred B. Leadership among pre-school children. *J. Abn. Soc. Psychol.*, 1933, 27, 430–440.

11. Tannenbaum, R., and Schmidt, Warren H. How to choose a leadership pattern. *Harvard Business Review*, March-April, 1958, 96.

The success of the American free enterprise system has been attributed to the role of competition in society. Similarly, athletic endeavor is invariably permeated with competition. Competitive behavior seems a relatively ingrown part of personality. Infants a few months old have been observed to vie for the privilege of manipulating an object placed between them. Animals in societies relatively low on the evolutionary ladder frequently evidence behavior which can be classified as competitive.

The introduction of competition into a situation in which gross motor performance is taking place has an effect similar to that produced by the presence of an observer or some other kind of stressful event—the performer's tension level is raised. Competition can usually be counted upon to produce more forceful efforts which the performer will tend to endure for a more prolonged period of time.

Competition is usually viewed as more satisfying than cooperative performance even though, under competitive circumstances, the individual or group may not win. In sports contests as well as in low organizational games, the child must integrate competitive and cooperative behavior at the same time. He must cooperate with teammates in order to compete successfully with another group.

The statements which follow are primarily gleaned from literature in the field of social psychology. Many of these statements are closely related to others pre-

18 Competition

sented previously. Competition within and between groups frequently alters their cohesion, the group's status hierarchy, and other characteristics of social interactions.

141.0   *Inter-group competition frequently alters the groups' characteristics* (10).

Corollary 141.1   Successful competition by a team enhances the members' mutual attraction (6, 10).

Corollary 141.2   Competition, whether successful or not, is likely to enhance rather than detract from group cohesion (6).

Repeated reference in the literature is made to the apparently satisfying nature of competition, regardless of the amount of success this striving may elict. The numerous ways in which individuals can compete in physical skills are constantly apparent. Therefore, these findings suggest that competition enhances to a large degree the attractiveness of participation in physical activity.

Implications.   The physical educator has a powerful tool at his disposal insofar as he can, to some extent, regulate the amount of competition and the form it takes. It would thus seem important to channel competitive energies in constructive ways.

Physical activities are valued because, among other things, they offer the youth constructive and socially approved ways for releasing basic competitive drives which otherwise may be misdirected. Mere participation does not seem enough. This participation, to be completely satisfying, must result in the chance of winning some kind of struggle. It is frequently observed, for example, that if the situation does not obviously call for competitive behavior, individuals will create competition in order to satisfy this basic need.

Corollary 141.3   Competition will begin to appear between group members who are supposedly cooperating to beat a common foe (1).

Further evidence related to the satisfying nature of competition is obtained from investigation which finds that two individuals within apparently cooperating groups will frequently begin either obviously or subtly to vie with each other.

142.0   *The occurrence of competitive behavior is related to the competencies of the individuals or groups confronting one another* (3, 8, 9).

One investigator has placed the ratio between the perceived abilities of two people from 65:100 to 75:100 before competition will begin to occur.

Implications. The physical educator should learn, as horse handicap-pers have long ago, that before competition will occur he must in some way arrange conditions which will encourage individuals or teams to be-lieve that they have a reasonable chance of winning. If this is not accom-plished, several things may happen: (*a*) the individuals or teams may refuse to compete, (*b*) they may play together without keeping any kind of score, or (*c*) they may figure out ways of handicapping themselves.

One investigator has indicated that, for competition to occur, two in-dividuals must want the same thing at the same time and each must perceive himself as possessing the capabilities to obtain it. If the two com-batants do not perceive themselves as having a reasonable chance at com-peting successfully, it can be predicted that all-out efforts will not be evidenced.

143.0   *Competitive behavior is part of the individual's total per-sonality complex (4, 11).*

Corollary 143.1   Individuals tend to perceive others as competitive if they themselves are competitive in nature (4).

Corollary 143.2   Success in competition is based upon the individual's gen-eral level of anxiety as well as his needs for achievement.

Individuals with low levels of anxiety and high needs for achievement will usually improve their performance under competitive circumstances. People with a high level of anxiety and a high need for achievement will generally suffer performance decrements when faced with competitive circumstances.

Implications. Anxiety level, needs for achievement, and similar traits must be assessed in order to determine the manner in which an individual or group of individuals will function under competitive circumstances. An inexperienced coach, believing he has prepared a team for their first game of the season, has often met with these realities. Competition raises tension levels. If these levels are already at their optimum for effective performance, performance will suffer under competitive circumstances.

Corollary 143.3   Competition causes fluctuations in an individual's aspira-tion level (13).

Further evidence of the manner in which competition influences per-formance as a function of personality is the manner in which an individ-ual's self-estimates tend to become less accurate under competitive cir-cumstances.

Whether voiced inaccurate estimates of expected performance are intended to bluff the antagonist, or whether an individual's self-concept relative to physical performance tends to become out of focus when competing, is difficult to say. Nevertheless, the interaction of competition and aspiration level holds important implications for the physical educator and coach.

144.0   *Competition will significantly alter fitness test scores (12).*

Competition of various types, either real or imagined by the performers, will significantly influence fitness test scores. Fitness tests are usually composed of direct, forceful acts and/or tasks which evaluate endurance, both of which usually evidence significant improvement under competitive circumstances.

Scores on fitness tests are primarily a function of the social context in which they are given, rather than any objective measurement of muscular strength or cardio-vascular endurance. Unless such conditions as competition are controlled, the scores obtained in these test batteries are relatively meaningless.

Many times this is difficult because, even if boys are tested individually, they may feel that others will ultimately obtain knowledge of their scores. The effect of various kinds of social motives upon fitness testing is usually more marked in boys between the ages of 8 and 15.

145.0   *The appearance of competitive behavior is partly dependent upon the socio-economic class of the individual or group participating (1).*

Lower income groups will compete for different reasons and in different situations than will more privileged groups. If individuals are in the extreme upper or lower income levels, less competitive behavior will usually be evidenced, as they usually feel that their positions are relatively fixed and, despite best or worst efforts, they cannot improve or lower their rankings in society.

Generally, the middle class individual will evidence the most competitive behavior in the widest variety of situations. The lower class person will tend to feel that the odds are stacked against him and gravitate toward games of chance, in which his chances of winning are not so biased. The upper class individual will tend to believe that, no matter what the quality of his physical performance, his position is relatively secure.

Implications. Coaches and physical education teachers in various parts of the community can usually attest to the truth of the above statement. To expect highly competitive behavior from certain segments of society is simply not realistic. However, individuals in the lower economic groups may frequently judge success in physical endeavors as one of the few avenues which will raise their economic position in society, and thus they will work hard at competitive athletics.

Summary

Competition is a widespread and satisfying part of the performance of physical skills. It is usually productive of better group and individual effort in simple, forceful acts, while at times it may disrupt the scores produced in complex perceptual-motor skills.

Whether or not competition occurs, and to what degree, depends upon the personality of the performers, their socio-economic levels, the perceived "closeness" of the competitors, and the extent to which prior success or failure has been met in competitive circumstances.

BIBLIOGRAPHY

1. Allport, Gordon, Murphy, Gardner, and May, Mary. Memorandum on research in competition and cooperation. New York: Social Sciences Research Council, 1937.
2. Berridge, Harold L. An experiment in the psychology of competition. *Res. Quart.*, 1945, 16, 37–42.
3. Buhler, Charlotte. Die ersten sozialen Verhaltungsweisen des Kindes, in sociologische und psychologische Studien über das erste Lebensjahr. *Quell. u. Stud. z. jugendk.*, 1927, 5, 1–102.
4. Ferguson, L. W. The cultural genesis of masculinity-femininity. *Psychol. Bull.*, 1941, 38, 584–585.
5. Greenberg, Pearl T. Competition in children: an experimental study. *Amer. J. Psychol.*, 1932, 44, 221–248.
6. Grossack, M. H. Some effects of cooperation and competition on small group behavior. *J. Abn. Soc. Psychol.*, 1954, 49, 341–348.
7. Kohler, O. Über den Gruppenwirkungsgrad der menschlichen Körperarbeit und die Bedingung optimaler Kollektivkraftreaktion. *Indus. Psychotech.*, 1927, 4, 209–226.
8. Moede, W. *Experimentelle Massenpsychologie.* 1920.
9. ———. Der Wetteifer, Seine Struktur und sein Ausmass. *Zeit. Psych. pas Psych.*, 1920, 15, 353–368.
10. Myers, A. Team competition, success, and the adjustment of group members. *Abn. Soc. Psychol.*, 1962, 65, 325–332.
11. Ryan, E. Dean. Competitive performance in relation to achievement motivation and anxiety. Paper presented to the National Convention of the

American Association of Health, Physical Education and Recreation, Minneapolis, Minnesota, 1963.

12. Strong, Clinton H. Motivation related to performance of physical fitness tests. *Res. Quart.*, 1963, 34, 497–507.

13. Sutton-Smith, B., and Roberts, J. M. Rubrics of competitive behavior. *J. Genet. Psychol.*, 1964, 105, 13–37.

14. Triplett, N. The dynamogenic factors in pace-making and competition. *Amer. J. Psychol.*, 1898, 9, 507–533.

part seven

THE SUPERIOR AND
THE INFERIOR PERFORMER

Throughout recorded history, scholars have been interested in the psyche of the athlete. Greek philosophers linked their athletes closely to their gods, and suggested that athletic excellence implied a kind of spiritual purity. More recently, experimental psychologists and neo-freudian psychoanalysts have attempted to determine some of the parameters of high level physical skill.

One spurious assumption sometimes voiced is that eliciting superior athletic performance is solely a problem of psychologically preparing the athlete. Ignored is the indication that superior athletes probably possess innate perceptual-motor attributes somehow different from those of the mediocre performer. If a group of people are subjected to the same practice conditions, influenced by the personality of the same coach, and encouraged to persist in their efforts by the same kinds of motivating conditions, their final performances will differ widely.

Despite the fact that individual differences in neuromotor makeup influence performance in basic ways, the kind of environment in which the athlete practices, the dynamics of interactions between teammates, and the personal attributes of the performer himself all influence the quality and quantity of effort he will put forth. The athlete's stable personal characteristics, as well as the influence of relatively transitory factors, will significantly affect his performance. On the following pages some of these factors are explored.

19 The Superior Athlete

Three types of variables will be considered in these pages: (*a*) personality traits usually found in superior athletes, (*b*) desirable behavior on the part of the coach when interacting directly with the athlete, and (*c*) the general psychological environment in which the athlete trains and competes.

Most of the statements in the previous chapters, if applied, will tend to enhance performance. Some of these will be restated in this chapter for emphasis, while others will deal specifically with the superior athlete. Relatively few psychological studies have been carried out with their focus on what makes the superior athlete, although nearly every coach is quick to describe his particular psychology. The writer is aware of only one or two individuals in the United States whose primary research interests are directed toward the superior athlete, his personality, and performance. In Europe and South America, however, there are numerous others. In many cases their observations are usually gleaned from clinical observations of athletes undergoing psychoanalysis.

There are several blocks to productive research into the question of superior athletic performance, including, initially, the problem of defining an "athlete." Therefore, the statements which follow are more inferential than exact. It is hoped that consideration of these will prompt some readers not only to think more precisely about this kind of problem, but encourage them to permit their athletes to become the subjects of more definitive investigations.

Initially, we will consider the personality of the athlete, the traits which seem to accompany superior physical performance, and the personal feelings and fears of some individuals as they compete. One reasonable way to approach psychological preparation of the athlete is from a negative standpoint—what one can do to remove various psychological blocks to performance. It is from this standpoint that we begin our discussion.

146.0 *The removal of various fears in training and in competition seems imperative to the production of superior athletic competence.*

Corollary 146.1   The fear of failure is an important block to competitive behavior; the athlete who never commits himself to all-out effort in practice and in the game may be afraid of losing, rather than of any physical discomfort or harm.

Frequently, this fear is evidenced by superior performers who only practice or engage in solitary activities without ever testing themselves in competition, joining the team, or otherwise placing themselves in a position to risk failure. This kind of behavior may be evidenced by athletes who have basic insecurities gained from other life experiences. Some athletes seem to turn to athletics as a kind of catharsis, and may not wish to risk further failure in this haven they have have constructed for themselves.

One of the most frustrating experiences for a coach is to be aware of marked athletic potential which lies relatively dormant because of an individual's refusal to go out for the team. The writer, then a swimming coach, and a colleague, coaching track at a small college several years ago, wrote an article in the school paper about "dormitory athletes" who, because of frequent bragging about their athletic prowess, should band together and form "athletic teams." It was further suggested that these boys meet on a "lounge-to-lounge" basis, tell each other about their potential successes, and decide individual and team winners by discussion. They would, of course, not need coaches, only public relations experts, they could wear smoking jackets rather than lettermen sweaters, and would immediately be declared ineligible if found near the athletic field or swimming pool.

While the humor in the article was primarily enjoyed by the writers rather than by the recipients of the barbs, it would have probably been more productive to have attempted to find why boys with superior athletic records in high school were refusing to place themselves in positions which would require sustained effort.

A number of approaches may be made to such individuals. They might be made consciously aware of their fear of failure. Bringing these feelings to their attention may help overcome them. The character-building function of meeting one's fears directly might be stressed. Many such boys really do not know their potential excellence. Giving them accurate information as to what they may expect from athletic participation would seem helpful under these circumstances.

Corollary 146.2   **Fear of winning is another block to superior athletes who, although able to win, stop just short of ultimate success.**

Most athletes will hotly deny intentionally "throwing" a game. When some athletes are subjected to in-depth analysis, it has been found that they are failing to win even though it is obviously within their capacities.

Some athletes have been identified, for example, as failing to win because they are under more pressure than is comfortable. If they win they will need to practice longer, to strive harder in future competitive situations. Everyone loves an underdog to win when it is unexpected, but the consistent winner is usually the "bad guy," and many individuals and teams unconsciously refuse to assume such a role.

Some fears of winning have been attributed directly to the feelings teams and individuals have about their coaches or fans. If there is a deep-seated dislike for the coach and/or others who stand to enhance their personal prestige through victories, athletes will at times not perform to their potential, will court failure, and in other ways not achieve up to their potential in conscious and unconscious efforts to punish the non-working members of their athletic community.

It is doubtful that this kind of block to performance can be verbalized or identified without prolonged therapy of some kind. Group therapy has sometimes been successful in some cases of this nature. After prolonged exposure to this kind of probing, the subtle "fear of winning" can often be exposed and corrected. The individual who fails when he can win in order to punish others or to keep pressure away from his subsequent performances is beginning a chain of behavior which can have serious effects upon his intellectual functioning in a number of problem-solving situations. Unless this is corrected, it could influence his professional and vocational performance away from the athletic field.

Corollary 146.3   Fear of pain is a frequent block to superior achievement in sports.

This third fear is important to consider when attempting to train the athlete for prolonged performance in swimming, running and similar sports. Numerous track coaches have suggested that overcoming fear of pain is the biggest step toward the production of a superior track athlete. Accomplishing this, however, is sometimes difficult.

Pain is a subjective phenomenon. Conditions which hurt some people are ignored by others. Pain has at times been objectified by having people fill out questionnaires concerning the intensity of a pain that they experience, i.e., at what point does it fall on a ten point scale? Another approach to the study of pain in athletes is to apply some kind of painful stimulus, such as an electric shock or a sharp cleat, and record the intensity of pain the individual can stand before asking for it to be removed. Both of these approaches, of course, have their advantages and drawbacks.

These studies are beginning to demonstrate that athletes somehow seem to reduce the amount of pain they experience, particularly in contact sports. Whether individuals impervious to pain seek contact sports or whether continual participation in pain producing sports raises the threshold to pain is unclear.

A second kind of pain is experienced in practice as the individual places excessive demands upon his cardio-respiratory system. Some individuals, upon experiencing pain when finishing a race, will tend to lag in subsequent races so as not to incur this kind of unpleasantness again. On the other hand, the superior athlete will be aware of how much it will hurt when fully extending himself, and somehow refuses to let it worry him.

It is believed that the coach should, in endurance workouts, tell individuals on the team that extending oneself to the ultimate is the only way now known to improve endurance performance. The body will accommodate this painful overload, and over-all improvement will be evidenced if the individual does not "draw back" by refusing to "push" himself. Thus, as much as possible, the coach should make the athlete aware of the painful as well as the rewarding nature of athletics, and attempt to enable him to accommodate the pain inherent in the production of superior performance. The athlete should himself be aware that constant improvement, particularly in performances which require cardio-vascular endurance, inevitably involves some degree of pain.

147.0   Certain groups of personality traits are found in superior athletes. At times, certain clusters of traits are specific to various sports.

Superior athletic performance is usually achieved by individuals with a background of success which has elicited a generally high need for achievement with accompanying high aspiration level. Athletes are usually interested in constantly exploring their potential, and are thus involved a considerable part of the time in setting reasonable goals for themselves.

The personalities of most superior athletes are often marked by hostility and aggression, usually kept well under control and channeled into performance specialties. This aggression may be elicited by childhood experiences, as is claimed by several European psychoanalysts who have studied the athletes of their countries, or by contemporary events in the lives of the performers.

At times, this hostility will be misdirected toward the coach or team members. It must be remembered that the problem is to redirect it, rather than crush it with excessive amounts of discipline, as is usually the reaction of a coach whose authority may be threatened in this way.

Athletes usually have an acute awareness of the social implications of their successes and/or failures; they are socially sensitive while they may or may not be socially outgoing. Good athletes are often extremely perceptive; they know their own physical and emotional limitations and attributes. At the same time, they are aware of the psychological makeup of those with whom they come in contact. The strivings of athletes in sports given widespread approval by the culture can usually be attributed largely to the social approbation forthcoming for superior achievement.

The social implications for failure are well known to the athlete and have been referred to previously in the text. The superior athlete is usually motivated by both negative and positive social attitudes, the potential disapproval as well as the approval which may be evidenced by those within his social context. Part of the coach's job is to utilize these negative and positive motives constructively to attune the tension level of the athlete to the specific tasks facing him.

The coach also has the obligation of aiding the high striving athlete to set goals he is capable of obtaining, so that, with frequent success, his aspiration remains high. Continual overmatching of an athlete or athletic team against opponents or goals which are too high would seem to detract from this desirable personality trait.

These same personality attributes have been noted in women athletes. Some European scholars have identified a syndrome of traits in women which they have termed the "Diana Complex." It has been assumed that this kind of striving nature is desirable in women athletes, and psychoanalysts have set about the problem of understanding it as related to feminine sports performers.

148.0   *Certain personality traits have been identified as desirable in superior coaches.*

Corollary 148.1   It is difficult for a sensitive, interested coach to remove himself emotionally from the performance of athletes he has prepared for competition. Physiological measures obtained simultaneously from performing athletes and their observing coaches are usually similar.

Similar to the personality traits of their athletes, superior coaches are also competitive in nature and have high needs for achievement and high aspiration levels. They are not satisfied with mediocrity or less than optimum performance from athletes in their charge. A superior coach combines technical knowledge with sensitivity; he is sensitive to the needs and attitudes of his athletes and, in constructive ways, attempts to mold their value systems.

From a technical standpoint, the coach is aware of current theories of learning, transfer, and particularly of the advisability of spacing practice when performance increments are not evidenced. The primary way for a coach to elicit respect from his athletes is to possess an inexhaustible knowledge of the sport, from mechanical principles governing the performance of specific sub-skills to knowledge of team strategy. This technical know-how should be based on a scientific approach to problem-solving, rather than folk-lore or "truth by proclamation."

The coach should always seek to impart his knowledge of the technical nature of the activity to his athletes. The athlete should be approached at his uppermost level of understanding. Superior athletes are scholars of their sports, and the proficient coach should assist the athlete in this quest for knowledge. Information should come in the form of general facts concerning the nature of physiological change during exercise as well as various psychological parameters of performance important to the athlete. The athlete should be assisted in learning about his own psychological makeup and the reasons he is competing and participating in the activity.

Furthermore, the coach and athlete should concern themselves with analyses of the psychological makeup of their opponents. Exploiting temperament weaknesses of one's opponents is a time-honored way of winning a game.

149.0 *Psychological variables influencing the total training and competitive environment should be controlled to offer the athlete optimum conditions in which to achieve excellence.*

The training environment should provide conditions which place intense stress upon the athlete so as to prepare him for the ultimate stress of competition. Physical and intellectual change involve accommodation to stressors in a classroom or on the athletic field. For the coach to fail to provide circumstances which encourage this desired change is to fail the highly competitive athlete. Respect and satisfaction are gained from athletics if participants are pleased with their over-all performance and achievements at the banquet at the end of the season or when receiving their grades from a course instructor after a tough semester. Attempting to make steps to this ultimate success by simply holding easy practices during the season is not sound.

150.0 *The practice situation should be flexible and ever-changing.*

The perceptive coach should provide a practice environment in which the athlete has various demands placed upon him on different days, or the same demands appearing in different forms. Throughout this text it has been emphasized that motivation arises from task complexity and novelty. For practices to be bland, routine, and never changing is to ignore one of the basic principles of motivation. Even though most athletes have strong internal reasons for achieving in sports, the importance of providing an environment which encourages maximum effort should not be neglected.

The exact parameters of each day's practice should be outlined for the athlete so he can pace himself. Exact goals should also be outlined prior to each competition. Reasonable, but high, expectations relative to individual and group performance should be stated clearly by the coach and accepted by the athlete prior to each athletic contest.

Individual differences in personality and ability can be accommodated when adhering to the above principle. Not only should workouts be flexible and vary from day to day, but at the same time they might be varied for each person on the team. This attention to deail on the part of the coach inspires confidence from his athletes, which is reflected not only in a desirable rapport being established but also in superior performances.

151.0   *Precise steps should be taken to exploit certain variables in the social climate in which the athlete trains and participates.*

Athletes in such individual sports as swimming and gymnastics should be brought together and made aware of the performance goals being set for each. Many times, in sports of this nature, feelings of teamwork have to be definitely planned for by use of techniques of this nature; if left to chance, they may never materialize.

Intersquad competitions which do not arise spontaneously may be planned by the coach. While intersquad rivalry may sometimes prove disrupting, at other times this kind of competition can be stimulating to an athletic team.

Team practices may be conducted in front of an audience to prepare team members for performance fluctuations they will experience in front of hostile and/or friendly fans. Simulated hostile audiences, for example, may be employed in an effort to give less experienced team members practice in performing under conditions of social stress.

Team leaders elected by the members should be given leadership training. Making such an individual more sensitive to the traits which elicit trust from his followers, and aware of the values and friendship hierarchy of the team, should make him a more effective team captain.

In the previous pages, only the surface of some of the psychological parameters of the coach-superior athlete relationship has been touched upon. It is these variables which are most meaningful to coaches, because they are the ones over which they have the most control.

It would seem athletic success is a combination of superior personality traits, inherent neuromotor makeup appropriate to the demands of the sport, and an environment which permits the athlete to train intensely and intelligently. Neglect of any one of these factors seems certain to produce an athlete working at less than his potential.

BIBLIOGRAPHY

Ogilvie, Bruce, and Tutko, Thomas A. *Problem athletes and how to handle them.* London: Pelham Books Ltd., 1966.

Within the past ten years, increasing emphasis has been placed upon identification and education of children at the opposite end of the continuum from the expert athlete. Certain children have been identified by the medical profession as evidencing a "clumsy child" syndrome. This syndrome alludes to a constellation of symptoms revolving around behavior which indicates mild to moderate perceptual-motor impairment. Some of these children can be classified as mentally retarded or educationally handicapped, while others seem to function well intellectually and evidence only movement problems.

These children may be characterized in several ways. They generally have a poor perception of their bodies, with particular difficulty noted when asked to make various left-right discriminations. At times, this kind of perceptual malfunction may be reflected in reading problems, as they seem unable to organize space well and may, for example, have difficulty discriminating between "b's" and "d's" or between the words "no" and "on."

They also have problems in trying to move their bodies accurately and quickly. Their reaction time is slow. They often evidence inappropriate gait patterns and are unable to hop, jump, or skip well. They may have difficulty integrating various parts of their bodies in skilled activities and do not, for example, utilize legs and body well when throwing, nor do they involve their arms properly when jumping.

20 The "Clumsy Child" Syndrome

Often these children have difficulty with hand-eye coordinations and manipulating small objects. Their handwriting is often poor. Other limitations are apparent as they attempt to catch balls. Not only can they frequently not track the ball well visually, but they also have difficulty moving hands and body in the correct way to intercept it as it arrives.

Emotional problems arise as the result of the child's ability to assess his ineptitudes by comparing his abilities with those evidenced by more competent children. Numerous authors have referred to the tendency of the slightly handicapped toward emotional problems caused by their inability to elicit proper help in the absence of constructive programs designed specifically for their needs.

In this increasingly affluent society, the more severe childhood maladies have been conquered to a large degree. As a result, pediatricians have begun to look at some of these more subtle childhood problems. Various training programs are being initiated throughout the nation for the kind of child who fails to make the Little League Baseball team or the Pop Warner Football Squad. As this kind of perceptual-motor problem is seen more frequently in children who also evidence mild to severe mental retardation, improvement in movement attributes is being looked upon by many clinicians as a means through which intellectual functioning may be improved (4, 5).

Several self-styled "educationalists" have put forth oversimplified theories of mental-visual-auditory training, heavily dependent upon practice of a few movements. A kind of recapitulation theory often seen in the writings of eighteenth and nineteenth century philosophers has begun to reappear in different garb. Rousseau, for example, suggested that the child progresses through stages similar to steps in the evolution of man, from the savage to the civilized city dweller. He wrote that the child appears first in the animal stage, passes through behavior evidenced by the savage, then to the pastoral stage, and finally achieves civilized status by reaching the social stage which terminates when he marries the ideal girl. Some of these neo-recapitulation theories parallel this, but pair child development with even earlier stages of evolution, comparing the child at various times in his life with fish, reptiles, and mammals. It has been suggested that the human nervous system is composed of discrete layers which can be specifically trained through motor activity. A kind of lamination theory of neuro-motor functioning and development has been proposed which could only be acceptable to neurologists of a century ago.

The research findings in child development, together with several theories espoused by reputable child psychologists, do contain principles worth considering. Evidence suggests that visual-motor integrations important in classroom learning may be enhanced through participation in activities resembling those usually found in physical education classes. It is believed that these principles can act as guidelines for programs in which the clumsy and/or retarded child may better realize his potential. It is our purpose in this chapter to outline some of these.

This writer believes that movement experiences are important for the establishment of early, basic perceptions formed by the child about himself, his world, and his relationship to this world. It is also believed that, later in life, certain motor experiences which involve the total child can aid *certain components* of the total educational process. However, the assertion that movement underlies *all the thought processes* seems a gross overstatement of the relationship between mental and motor functioning (6).

The total development of the retarded child who is in some ways similar to the infant in his neuro-motor makeup may be aided by exposing him to a variety of perceptual-motor experiences. Various facets of the educational process may be improved by constructing situations which require the child to become totally involved through movements of his large muscles. It is thus proposed that gross movement constitutes an important type of sensory experience which, together with other approaches, may be more thoroughly exploited in educational programs for atypical children.

152.0   *Children with slight to moderate perceptual deficiencies evidence discrete types of problems* (3).

Corollary 152.1   Careful assessment should precede the development of activities in educational programs.
Corollary 152.2   Activities of six or seven different types should be included in such programs, consisting of tasks designed to improve balance, agility, perception of body-parts, sports skills, and hand-eye coordination (2).

Statements presented in Chapter 1 suggest the specific nature of motor ability. Although this specificity is not usually as marked in retarded children or children with moderate motor handicaps, there is still a need to design programs of activities directed toward the improvement of specific attributes. It is wasteful of time and money to expose children who evidence problems only in manual dexterity, for example, to activities designed to improve their gait.

As a child is exposed to a variety of activities, improvement in some of them may transfer to others. Apart from the possibility of identical elements being present in two skills, as the child learns how to learn motor skills and begins to feel better about his abilities to accomplish *something* on the playground, a generalized success syndrome will elicit improvement in the performance of a variety of tasks.

153.0   *Gross actions usually involve the necessity of integrating data from several of the sensory end-organs.*

Corollary 153.1   The pairing of movement to vision may be practiced in a variety of ways, using motor skills of various kinds (5).

Asking the child to walk a balance beam while watching a stable point or a point moving in various relationships to him would be an important kind of experience to present to a child with motor problems. Crawling in itself may improve some of the basic locomotor patterns, but when paired with the necessity of placing the hands in colored "hands" on the floor, an even more helpful task involving visual-motor integrations is presented. These are a few of several ways a child can be assisted to coordinate his vision with his movements.

154.0   *Movement tasks can provide experiences which tend to focus the hyperactive child for increasingly longer periods of time (6).*

Hyperactivity is often evidenced by children diagnosed as brain-damaged. This syndrome is characterized by general perceptual disorganization and behavior which is similarly disorganized. This kind of child is constantly in motion, and rarely manages to concentrate for a reasonable period of time on anything. The impediment of this kind of behavior to classroom learning is obvious.

Within a distraction-free environment, movement tasks can be utilized in an attempt to maintain such a child's attention to a given job for increasingly longer periods of time. For example, a balance beam can be placed in the center of an otherwise empty room. When the child is able to maintain his attention on the beam while traversing its entire length, a second beam can be added to the end of this one and the process continued. Obstacle courses can also be utilized to attempt to improve attention span. Training of this kind assumes that, if the child can be taught to concentrate on a task for a period of time longer than he has attended to anything before, some of this decrease in distractibility may transfer to the classroom.

This kind of training has to be carried out with tasks of exactly the correct degree of difficulty; at the same time, they must frequently be modified and changed. The hyperactive child has little tolerance for the too difficult or the too easy, and usually fails to attempt problems which he perceives as too threatening or too simple.

155.0   *Form recognition may be aided by participation in various playground activities (1).*

Corollary 155.1   The recognition of simple geometric patterns must precede the recognition of letters and the development of the ability to block print letters.

Playground activities are usually planned on squares and circles. It would seem helpful to the child who has difficulty recognizing simple geometric shapes basic to letter formation to practice games on triangles, hexagons, half-circles, and so on. This practice could take place in the form of an organized game, or might consist of walking, hopping, or otherwise moving around the periphery of these shapes. Verbalization concerning the shape can probably accompany this kind of practice.

Additional activities can be carried out on large letters drawn on the playground. A grid composed of squares in which letters of the alphabet are placed can be turned into a spelling game as the child attempts to spell words by jumping in letters in the correct serial order.

Further practice in pattern recognition could take place with the construction of playground apparatus suitable for climbing. The child could explore and verbalize about his experiences while climbing the letters "A" and "B," for example. These activities should not replace traditional classroom experiences intended to promote the same abilities, but could enhance certain perceptual attributes by supplementing the traditional classroom activities.

156.0   *The ability to order items in correct series may be gained by exposing a child to several movements involving correct ordering (6).*

Basic to spelling is the ability to order letters correctly in appropriate series. A number of motor tasks can be utilized to improve this kind of ability. In addition to the child being totally involved in the task is the advantage that the teacher-observer can assess exactly the relative success of the child's efforts.

A series of structured movements or obstacles to negotiate in a series can be gradually increased in length. After a child is able to remember two movements in a series, such as a jump and a hop into a circle, a third might be added, and then a fourth, and so on. Through these means, the ability to order letters correctly in series might also be improved.

157.0   *Movement experiences may help to heighten the child's perceptions of his body, the left-right dimensions of his body, and the position of his body relative to various objects (2, 5).*

Corollary 157.1   The child's body, particularly until the age of eight or nine, forms a basic frame of reference from which complex judgments in space are made (5).

Corollary 157.2 Basic to body part perception is the child's concept of left and right. One must have the ability to identify the left hand correctly and to realize that the left leg is on the same side of the body.

Several psychologists have proposed activities designed to enhance the child's perceptions of his body. Among these are games played while the child is on his back, moving his limbs in various ways and in various combinations while pressing them against the floor.

Others have suggested that the trampoline is an important developmental tool with which perceptions of the body can be heightened. Another exercise involves drawing around the child as he lies on his back, then permitting him to stand up and inspect his body outline.

As the child begins to appear able to organize his body surfaces and parts to some extent, additional tasks should be introduced which help him to perceive better his location relative to objects and the placement of objects relative to him. Initial training of this kind could include asking the child to arrange himself in various relationships to a box, e.g., "stand in front of it, put your left side toward it, put your back toward it." Similarly, the child in a fixed position could be asked to describe where objects are being placed relative to him, e.g., "it is in back of me, to my left-rear, right-front."

An adjunct to this kind of practice is the ability to discriminate correctly the left-right dimensions of objects and letters in space. Initial directionality training could consist of requiring the child to identify the body parts of an individual facing him or the body parts of a picture of a man. Such practice would require that the child project himself into the picture, and should enable him to perform better in the innumerable classroom tasks which require similar abilities.

158.0 Motor tasks may be arranged so that problem-solving behavior is required of children.

Recently, motor experiences have been used more and more by educational psychologists to enhance the problem-solving ability of children. Typical of the arrangements used is to present a child or group of children with simple objects, such as a ball (that doesn't roll very well), a cup, and a stick, and ask them to invent a game or games. The quantity and quality of creative thinking that can arise from this kind of situation is at times truly amazing. Most important, the evidence that problem-solving is taking place is concrete and observable by others.

159.0 When attempting to educate severely retarded children, one must start with basic experiences rather than classroom learning tasks (2).

Children of this type must first be helped to find out where they are and what they are doing. The use of basic motor activities outlined on the previous pages should certainly be a starting point for such children.

Summary

Tasks traditionally utilized only in physical education classes are being employed to a constantly greater degree to educate children with perceptual-motor problems of a mild to severe nature. Such experiences totally involve the child, requiring him to focus in an obvious way on the task and to involve many important kinds of visual-motor pairings.

Figure recognition, serial memory ability, and similar perceptual attributes may be enhanced by the proper kinds of motor tasks. Movement does not underlie all symbolic-cognitive thought, particularly after the age at which language develops. On the other hand, perceptual-motor experiences can aid the child who has deficiencies in his neuro-motor makeup, and can contribute importantly in other ways to the total educational program for infants, children, and youth.

BIBLIOGRAPHY

1. Cratty, Bryant J. Transfer of small-pattern practice to large-pattern learning. *Res. Quart.*, 1962, 33, 523–535.
2. ———. *Developmental sequences of perceptual-motor tasks.* Freeport, N.Y.: Educational Activities, Inc., 1967.
3. Cruickshank, William M., Benzen, Frances A., Ratzeburg, Frederick H., and Tannhauser, Miriam T. *A teaching method for brain-injured and hyperactive children.* Syracuse, N.Y.: Syracuse Univ. Press, 1961.
4. Delacato, Carl H. *The diagnosis and treatment of speech and reading problems.* Springfield, Illinois: Charles C. Thomas, 1964.
5. Kephart, Newell C. *The slower learner in the classroom.* Columbus, Ohio: Charles E. Merrill, 1956.
6. Los Angeles City Schools. A program of developmental physical education activities for educationally handicapped pupils. Special Education Branch, 1966, 75 pp. mimeo.
7. Mosston, Muska. *Teaching physical education.* Columbus, Ohio: Charles E. Merrill, 1966.
8. Robbins, Melvyn Paul. The Delacato interpretation of neurological organization. *Reading Res. Quart.*, Spring, 1966, 57–77.

Index